The mind in action

Cognitive science – which draws on ideas from psychology, philosophy, linguistics and artificial intelligence (AI) – attempts to explain our mental life within a scientific framework. Its goal is, thus, to remove the last major obstacle to a unified scientific account of the natural world. In *The Mind in Action*, Alan Garnham provides an invaluable introduction to this exciting new development in the study of mind.

The Mind in Action focuses on the development of a systematic explanation of cognition, rather than on facts about the way we perceive things, remember them, talk about them, think about them, and interact with them. Alan Garnham looks in detail at the nature of scientific explanations, the reasons for developing them, and the way they are assessed. He describes the work carried out by cognitive scientists and considers the questions that motivate it. He introduces the computational metaphor for the mind, and explains how flushing out that metaphor might lead to an integrated scientific account of mental phenomena.

Designed primarily for people about to embark on courses in cognitive science and related disciplines, *The Mind in Action* captures the liveliness and excitement of debates about the mind. It is readily accessible to anyone with an interest in how the mind works, avoiding technical terms where possible and explaining them fully where they are necessary.

Alan Garnham is Lecturer in Experimental Psychology, University of Sussex, and author of *Psycholinguistics: Central Topics* and *Artificial Intelligence: An Introduction.*

The mind in action

A personal view of cognitive science

Alan Garnham

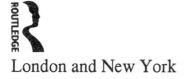

London and New York

First published 1991
by Routledge
11 New Fetter Lane, London EC4P 4EE

Simultaneously published in the USA and Canada
by Routledge
a division of Routledge, Chapman and Hall, Inc.
29 West 35th Street, New York, NY 10001

Typeset by Michael Mepham, Frome, Somerset
Printed and bound in Great Britain by
Mackays of Chatham PLC, Chatham, Kent

British Library Cataloguing in Publication Data
Garnham, Alan *1954* –
    The mind in action: a personal view of
    cognitive science.
    1. Man. Cognition
    I. Title
    153.4

Library of Congress Cataloging in Publication Data
Garnham, Alan, 1954 –
    The mind in action: a personal view of cognitive
    science/Alan Garnham.
    p.   cm.
    Includes bibliographical references and index.
    1. Cognitive science. 2. Cognition. 3. Intellect. 4. Artificial
    intelligence. I. Title
    BF311.G35   1991
    153–dc20   90-47508
                                                        CIP

ISBN 0-415-00848-4
ISBN 0-415-00849-2 (pbk)

To Jane

Contents

Figures

Acknowledgements

Routledge gratefully acknowledges permission to reproduce in *The Mind in Action* by Alan Garnham material previously published elsewhere. Harcourt Brace Jovanovitch Inc allowed use of figure 4.2 (figure 2.6 in this volume) from *Human Information Processing*, second edition. The Royal Society of London, H.K. Nishihara and E. Hildreth granted permission for reproduction of figure 8 (figure 2.3) from 'Representation and recognition of the spatial organisation of three-dimensional shapes', from *The Proceedings of the Royal Society of London*, series B. The Royal Society of London and E. Hildreth allowed use of figure 6 (figure 2.1) from 'The theory of edge detection', from *The Proceedings of the Royal Society of London*, series B. The Macmillan Publishing Company granted permission to reproduce figure 22 (figure 7.1) from *The Cerebral Cortex of Man* by W. Penfield and T. Rasmussen. The AFIPS Press allowed use of figure 19 (figure 2.4) from 'Decomposition of a visual field into three-dimensional bodies', which appeared in *AFIPS Proceedings of the Fall Joint Computer Conference*, vol. 33. The Academic Press and T. Winograd allowed use of figure 3 (figure 1.2) from 'Understanding natural language', *Cognitive Psychology*, 3. Every effort has been made to obtain permission to reproduce copyright material throughout this book. If any proper acknowledgement has not yet been made, the copyright holder should contact the publisher.

Preface

Over the last few hundred years science has made enormous advances. In the last century the theory of evolution removed one of two major obstacles to a unified scientific account of the natural world. It showed how the origins of life could be explained. Cognitive science attempts to remove the last of these barriers. Its aim is to explain within a scientific framework (at least some aspects of) our mental life.

This book introduces cognitive science *as a science*. It focuses on the development of a systematic explanation of cognition, rather than on interesting facts about the way we perceive things, remember them, talk about them, think about them, and interact with them. To give a feel for what cognitive scientists are trying to do, it looks in detail at the nature of scientific explanations, the reasons for developing them, and the way they are assessed. More particularly, the book introduces the computational metaphor for the mind, and explains how that metaphor, or rather the fleshing out of that metaphor, plays a central role in integrating an account of mental phenomena into a broadly mechanistic scientific framework.

I have written the book in a way that should be readily accessible to anyone with an interest in how the mind works, avoiding technical terms where possible and explaining them fully where they are necessary. I hope that the book will also be of interest to A-level students of psychology and related disciplines, to people considering cognitive science or one of its sub-disciplines as a university or polytechnic course, and to those who have already embarked on such a course. However, the book is in no sense a textbook. Indeed, I have tried to capture the excitement of cognitive science, which many introductory texts seem to miss. Although my coverage is wide-ranging, it is by no means systematic, and it is very far from complete. The book presents a personal view – another author would have written about different issues. However, I hope my readers will look elsewhere for more information and for different perspectives. To start them on what I hope will be a lengthy trail I have suggested a small number of books as further reading at the end of most chapters.

My thanks go to Jane Oakhill for her detailed comments on and discussion of an earlier draft, to George Mather for producing figure 2.2, to Mary Ann Kernan for encouraging me to write the book, and to David Stonestreet, Rowena Gaunt and Christine Winters for seeing the manuscript through its subsequent stages.

1   Introduction

It is a typical morning and I am sitting at the breakfast table. I reach over and take a piece of toast from the toast rack, look around for the marmalade pot, which I don't see at first because it is not in its usual place. I try to start a crossword puzzle, and because I'm concentrating on a difficult anagram I do not hear a request to pass the butter. As I finish my coffee, I try to remember my duties and appointments for the day.

What could be more commonplace? There is nothing in need of an explanation here, surely. Or if there is, the explanation will be entirely straightforward. How come I have appointments and duties? Well, I work at the university and it is a weekday in term time. Surely no other kind of explanation of what is happening is required! There's no room for a *scientific* explanation of anything happening here!

One of my main aims in this book is to show that abilities most of us are able to take for granted – for example those I exercised at the breakfast table – can be the subject of scientific investigation. And not only can they be investigated, trying to explain them is one of the most exciting and difficult challenges that modern science can offer. Among these abilities are the ability to recognise an object in a scene in front of us, the ability to produce and understand spoken and written language, the ability to reach out for and manipulate objects with our hands, the ability to solve problems such as anagrams, the ability to remember. I hope to show what a scientific explanation of such abilities is, in what ways it is like and in what ways different from an everyday explanation, and what benefits such an explanation confers on us.

The science in which these abilities are studied is called *cognitive science* – the science of cognition. *Cognition*, according to the Penguin dictionary, is 'the faculty of knowing and perceiving'. That faculty is highly developed in humans and developed to a lesser extent in other animals. Knowing and perceiving require attending to things, remembering them, thinking about them, making judgements about them and talking, writing and reading about them. These abilities are, therefore, all studied in cognitive science. Traditionally, cognition is contrasted with two other faculties of the mind: conation, the exercise of the will, and affection, the experience of feelings and emotions. In fact, it is difficult to maintain a clear distinction between these three aspects of mental life. Both feeling and willing have a cognitive component. Nevertheless, scientists have to subdivide difficult problems – such as understanding the mind – and it makes pragmatic sense to focus on the problems of cognition in a discipline called cognitive science.

Cognition is a faculty that can be turned on itself, as the biblical injunction to know thyself indicates. People have a natural propensity to want to explain things, including their own behaviour and other people's. However, any phenomenon can be explained in several, not necessarily incompatible, ways. In particular, there can be both everyday and scientific explanations of people's behaviour, and those two types of explanation need not be incompatible. Some of our cognitive abilities have everyday explanations and others do not. However, it does not follow that there cannot be or need not be scientific explanations of those abilities. There is no reason why such explanations should not be developed – no reason why there should not be a cognitive science.

The name *cognitive science* is a relatively new one. The reason is not that people have only just started studying cognition scientifically. Far from it. Cognition has been studied in many academic disciplines. But it is only recently that people with different viewpoints have decided that they ought to pool their methods and resources to attack what are very difficult problems. In particular, cognition has been studied scientifically in psychology, artificial intelligence, linguistics and anthropology. In addition, some philosophical ideas about cognition contribute to cognitive science. To take just one example, philosophers who study logic worry about what makes an argument valid. So their ideas might be either directly or indirectly relevant to theories about how people reason.

This introductory chapter has two purposes. First, it discusses what a scientific explanation is, and how it differs from an everyday explanation. This discussion indicates what explanations in cognitive science are like and what they are good for. Second, it introduces very briefly some ways of studying cognition scientifically.

Before turning specifically to *cognitive* science, it's worth stopping to think more generally about how scientific explanations and everyday explanations are related. This exercise will suggest what a scientific explanation of, say, the ability to recognise common objects might be like. It is not necessary to know much about science in order to understand what follows. Indeed, I will consider a very simple example, understanding how a vacuum cleaner works. A lot of readers will probably think: I don't know anything about how vacuum cleaners work! But, of course, that's not true. If that was your reaction it must be because you think that what you know isn't worth mentioning, perhaps because it's so obvious. If you want to find someone who knows nothing (or almost nothing) about vacuum cleaners you'll have to look for, say, a Kalahari bushman. Almost every adult in our culture knows such facts as: vacuum cleaners are powered by electricity, they need to be plugged into the mains and switched on, they suck dirt out of carpets, which is collected in a bag and eventually thrown away. What we know about electricity also helps us to understand how vacuum cleaners work. For example, an electrical appliance will not work if its fuse has blown or if there is a loose wire in the plug.

The ideas that ordinary people have about vacuum cleaners, and about electricity in general, can be said to form a *folk theory* of how vacuum cleaners work. This term is not intended to be disparaging. Folk theories guide our interaction with the world, helping us in this case, for example, to get the cleaning done. Well-established folk theories are often essentially correct. And the more directly those theories guide our actions, the more likely they are to be right – we soon find out if our actions do not lead to the expected results. Interestingly, people's more abstract understanding of electricity, which is based on metaphors such as flowing water or teeming crowds, can incorporate fundamental misconceptions, which are hard to correct because their effect on everyday behaviour is indirect.

To say that a theory is a *folk* theory is to say it is part of our ordinary culture, and not restricted to a small class of experts. To say that it is a *theory* means that it is not simply a set of facts, but a set of general principles that generates specific explanations of how to go about cleaning a particular room, or of why a particular vacuum cleaner doesn't work on a particular occasion. So, if my vacuum cleaner does not start when I switch it on, I check that it is plugged in, that the socket is switched on, that the fuse has not blown, that there is no loose wire in the plug, and so on. For most people, myself included, the folk theory says: lots of things can (but rarely do!) go wrong with vacuum cleaners, but there is nothing I can do about them myself.

There is one more important point about our folk theory of vacuum cleaners. It is a theory that has developed in a world where vacuum cleaners are expected to work. If I plug in and switch on and the vacuum cleaner works, there is nothing to be explained. If it doesn't, and my simple trouble-shooting tricks fail, the explanation is that it needs mending.

What have vacuum cleaners got to do with cognitive science? Five points emerge from our discussion so far. First, we are constantly explaining why things happen or do not happen. It is a basic human instinct to try to explain things. Second, everyday explanations are typically required only when something unexpected happens. Indeed, another remarkable human characteristic is the ability to take for granted things that happen all the time. This characteristic partly explains why it can be difficult to see what a science of cognition might explain – we are so accustomed to people seeing things, understanding what is said to them, and performing other cognitive tasks. But all of these skills turn out to be complex once we start analysing them from a scientific point of view. Third, our explanations are based on what we expected to happen (but did not) and on the reasons why we expected it to happen (our folk theory of how vacuum cleaners work). Fourth, what needs to be explained depends on our purposes. If all goes according to plan (the vacuum cleaner works) and we fulfil our aim (the carpets are cleaned) there is nothing to be explained. Fifth, most of us know that we do not fully understand how vacuum cleaners work. However, we do not worry about our ignorance because it does not usually stop us cleaning carpets. It is more difficult to see that there is something we do not understand about our cognitive abilities.

I want to emphasise one further point. All explanations come to an end. At some point we take things for granted and agree that no further explanation is required (or, in the case of scientific explanations, that none can be given at present). This aspect of explanations is related to their purpose-relativity. So, for example, we do not need an (everyday) explanation for why a vacuum cleaner will not work if the fuse is blown. It is just a fact that when an appliance's fuse blows, it does not work. The reason why explanation can stop here is that what we need to do to make the vacuum cleaner work (our purpose) is to relace the fuse. For other purposes, or if the new fuse also blows, we must look for a further explanation of why the fuse has blown.

Perhaps the most important of these points for showing the difference between everyday explanations and scientific explanations is that explanations are purpose-relative. People's everyday purposes are, for the most part, easy to identify, even if they are not always easy to empathise with. The 'purpose' of scientific explanations is harder to grasp, but we can begin to see what it might be by pursuing our discussion of vacuum cleaners. Scientific explanations allow us to do things that everyday explanations do not. If our purpose is to clean carpets, the folk theory of vacuum cleaners will suffice. But if our purpose is to design or repair vacuum cleaners we will need a more sophisticated theory of how they work, a theory that begins to look much more scientific than the folk theory of vacuum cleaners. This fact shows that behind an everyday phenomenon that we take for granted – the existence of machines for cleaning carpets – there is much to be explained. To make this point more vividly, there is (at least as far as our everyday explanations go) something *deeply mysterious* about vacuum cleaners. How can there be machines that clean carpets? What general principles explain the possibility of constructing such devices? Our folk theory provides no answers to these questions, it simply assumes that vacuum cleaners exist. Similarly, we might wonder how it is possible for, say, the rattling of air molecules against a thin membrane (the eardrum) to convey information about events on the far side of the world: how do we understand what a newsreader is saying to us? An important difference, however, is that unlike vacuum cleaners people are not designed, but are rather the products of evolution. We know (indeed, it's part of our folk theory) that vacuum cleaners were invented and that they were invented by someone who understood mechanical and electrical principles. We know there is a more detailed account of how vacuum cleaners work, even if we do not know what it is. It is less obvious, but nevertheless true, that there can be an account of how minds work that is quite different from our everyday explanations of people's behaviour. There is a parallel with folk theories of other naturally occurring phenomena, such as the weather or the behaviour of inanimate objects. We have folk theories about these things, but we recognise that scientists provide another type of account.

The design of vacuum cleaners is applied science, and I deliberately chose this example to illustrate the idea of a deeper level of explanation that was still relative to a concrete purpose. It is more difficult to say what purpose explanations in pure science are relative to. Indeed, one reason for formulating scientific explanations is to create the most general kind of explanation possible.

EXPLANATIONS AND FACTS

What makes cognitive science exciting is that it allows us to develop a particular kind of explanation for certain phenomena, such as our ability to understand language and our ability to recognise objects. These phenomena are on the one hand commonplace, yet on the other hand deeply mysterious, partly because our everyday explanations take them for granted. It is, therefore, in the explanations (or theories) of cognitive science that its primary interest lies, *not in the facts it is trying to explain*. This is not to say that facts about our cognitive abilities are uninteresting. On the contrary, many of them are fascinating. For example, optical illusions, such as those illustrated in figure 1.1, are a source not only of amusement, but also of art, particularly in the work of M. C. Escher. And case histories, such as that of Clive Waring, subject of the television documentary *Prisoner of Consciousness*, can be not only interesting but also deeply moving. Waring is a musician who, after a viral infection of the brain, is unable to remember things that happened more than a few minutes ago. If his wife leaves the room for more than a few minutes he greets her as 'long lost' on her return. Yet his ability to conduct his choir remains virtually unimpaired. Illusions suggest theories

(a)

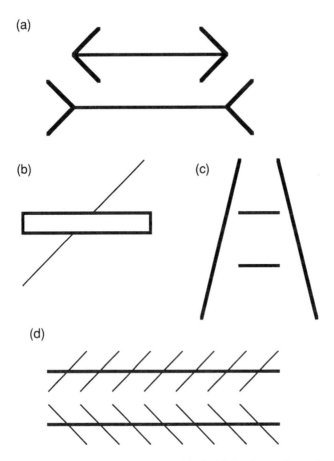

(b)

(c)

(d)

Figure 1.1 Some optical illusions. (a) The Müller-Lyer – the two horizontal lines are the same length. (b) The Poggendorf – the two sloping line segments are part of the same line. (c) The Ponzo – the two horizontal lines are the same length. (d) The Zöllner – the horizontal lines are parallel

about how the visual system works, and cases like Clive Waring lead to important insights about the organisation of our memories into separate compartments. However, for cognitive science, as opposed to general human curiosity, it is the theories not the facts that are of primary importance. Furthermore, a fact that may have no intrinsic interest may assume crucial importance, for example in deciding between two theories.

These observations explain why many people, including students of the subject, are disappointed by cognitive psychology. Psychologists emphasise experiments and their results (= facts), so people see cognitive psychology as being about matters that are inherently boring – how good people are at remembering different kinds of word list, for example. Students often favour topics such as social psychology or neuropsychology, in which the subject matter (the facts themselves) seems more interesting. A further problem arises because in those parts of psychology with inherently more interesting subject matter the construction of theories has proved difficult. Many so-called theories are little more than redescriptions of the facts. To the extent that other subdisciplines of cognitive science are more theoretically oriented, they are immune to such problems, but I suspect that they arise in linguistics and AI (Artificial Intelligence) as well.

However, *fact collecting is not science*. Nor is collecting of any sort. To be fascinated by the animal and plant kingdoms is to be interested in natural history, not to be a biologist. To collect gemstones is not to be a geologist. Similarly, human nature can be endlessly fascinating, but to know lots of interesting facts about cognition is not to be a cognitive scientist. Cognitive science is not about documenting the fascinating things that the human mind (or particular human minds) can or cannot do. It is about developing a framework within which we can explain the abilities we have.

Like other sciences, cognitive science starts with the desire for an explanation of those aspects of ordinary phenomena that everyday explanations leave unexplained. However, once a science gets under way two things happen. First, it takes on a life of its own and its connection with everyday concerns becomes less direct. Take physics, for example, which grew in part out of the desire to understand how arrows, cannonballs and other projectiles fly through the air or, in Newton's case, so legend has it, of why apples fall to the ground. The fact that apples fall is taken for granted in everyday explanations – we would only want an explanation if an apple went up. However, it rapidly became apparent that the way planets move, something that is far from everyday, was important for testing theories of motion and gravitation. Furthermore, physicists soon started talking about things much further from our everyday experience. Modern physics deals with strange objects such as quarks, of which ordinary people have only a very limited understanding.

Second, once a science has well-developed theories, any fact, however dull in itself, may become a test case for those theories. A scientist may set up an elaborate empirical investigation into something that seems boring in order to find out whether a particular theory is supported.

COGNITIVE SCIENCE

Let us return to cognition. Our folk theories of cognition, of what people see, hear, touch, taste, smell and feel and of what they know and how they know it, are, if anything, more elaborate than our folk theories of the physical world. The reason these theories, which are part of our *folk psychology*, are so well developed is that our interactions with the world and with other people are among the most important aspects of our lives. However, as our discussion of vacuum cleaners showed, folk psychology only makes sense against a background of what we expect to happen. Folk psychology need not provide explanations of what normally happens, since what is expected does not usually need to be explained.

Consider a particular example: the folk psychology of seeing. It would be impossible to detail everything a normal adult knows about seeing. There are basic facts, such as that people have two eyes on the front of their heads, that they see with their eyes and, hence, that people who have something wrong with their eyes are likely to have difficulty seeing. But there are other things: that spectacles can be used to correct certain types of poor sight, that things look bent in water, that it is more difficult to see in the dark. There are even genuinely folkloric elements to our folk theories: many people (though not readers of this book, of course) believe that eating carrots helps you see better in the dark. We also know that people with normal sight use that faculty to find out what is in their environment and to find their way around that environment. How do they do that? Here folk psychology cannot help. Its explanations end in facts that we all take for granted, such as that people (usually) see what is in front of their eyes. Folk psychology doesn't need an explanation of how they do so, and it hasn't developed one. As I have already hinted, there are various explanations for why this norm might not be met: it is dark, the person is blind, the person is experiencing an optical illusion. But we are never called on to explain why or, more importantly, *how* someone with normal sight in normal lighting conditions sees a table when they are looking at a table. The parallel with the vacuum cleaner example is clear. If all goes to plan, all you need to know to do the cleaning is the folk theory of vacuum cleaners plus some of the folk theory of electricity (it's usually available, if there's a power cut nothing will work etc.). You certainly don't need a scientific understanding of electricity. Similarly, to draw the right conclusions about what you see and what other people will be able to see, you just need the folk psychology of vision. That is sufficient for interacting successfully with other people – the purpose for which folk psychological explanations have developed. What people usually fail to realise is that, just as there is a scientific account of how electricity works, there can be a scientific account of how vision works. Part of the difficulty is that the *purpose* of the theory is not obvious. That is why people talk about scientific curiosity or the desire for knowledge. Scientific explanations have no immediate concrete purpose. Indirectly, however, they provide an understanding of the world, and an ability to control it, that other kinds of explanation do not.

Folk psychology tells us something about how the eyes work and thus hints at what a scientific theory of vision might have to explain. The cognitive science of vision is discussed in chapter 2, but I will briefly mention two aspects of it here. The first revolves around an apparent contradiction between two basic facts in the folk psychology of vision. One is that we have two eyes, each of which can be used on its own. When the head is still, they have slightly different views of the same scene, as closing each eye in turn shows. The other is that, under normal circumstances, when we look at a scene with two eyes open we see only a single view of it. This view is referred to as the cyclopean view, after the one-eyed monster of Greek mythology. It is a compromise between the two single-eyed views. A theory of vision will have to explain what advantage these two views provide (better perception of depth) and how the two views are combined into one.

The second example is that if you look inside an eye – and modern instruments such as the ophthalmoscope used in routine sight tests make this easy – you can see on the retina at the back of the eye an image of the scene that the eye is looking at. That image is *upside down*. Many people think this fact poses a problem. If the image is upside down, why doesn't the world look upside down? We know that it does not so, as cognitive scientists, we need a theory in which the fact that the image is upside down does not matter.

It is worth spending more time on this second example, because it illustrates a kind of theory that *cannot* provide a satisfactory explanation of cognitive functioning. Our feeling that the upside down image in the eye is a problem derives in part from our knowledge that if someone sees an upside down picture it looks upside down, and it is sometimes difficult to work out what it is a picture of. So if the theory of vision said: the way we see is that some part of the brain is like a little man looking at the images on the back of the eyes, that little man will have difficulty seeing those images properly, because they are upside down. This theory may seem crude and implausible, even risible, but similar ideas, in a more sophisticated form, have been proposed to account for our cognitive abilities. The little man in the head is called a *homunculus*, so the theories are called homunculus theories.

Cognitive science has no place for homunculus theories. The reason is not simply that a homunculus would have difficulty seeing upside down retinal images. There is a more serious problem with homunculus theories, and it is important to understand what that problem is. Homunculus theories *cannot* provide a scientific explanation of cognitive functioning. Let us stay with the homunculus theory of vision, though the argument applies to homunculus theories of any kind of cognitive functioning. We are trying to explain how the visual system works. The homunculus theory says that the way it works is by having another, similar, visual system inside it. But how does that visual system work? The so-called explanation leaves us with exactly the same question we started with: how does the visual system work? We have made no progress.

Whatever the explanations of cognitive science are like, they are not homunculus theories. If we are to explain cognition, we must not use our cognitive abilities themselves to explain it. So what sort of explanations are we going to provide?

The kind of explanations that cognitive scientists try to formulate are called *information processing* explanations. As will become apparent in the course of this book information processing explanations take different forms. For the present we will remain with our example of vision, and illustrate what such an explanation might look like. We saw that the homunculus theory is a non-explanation of our ability to see. Indeed, the kind of thinking that suggested the homunculus theory is based on a fundamental misconception of what vision entails. If we look into someone's eye with an ophthalmoscope, we see an image on the retina. However, we only see it as an image because our own visual system processes what is on the retina just as it processes anything else it sees. As far as the retina itself is concerned there is no image, just light falling on the so-called *receptor cells*. Indeed, one of the most important things that a theory of vision has to explain is how we get from the information available at the retina to an interpretation of that information in terms of objects in a scene.

So, the first thing we need to do in developing an information processing account of vision is to decide what information the visual system has to work on, in technical terms what its *input* is. In the case of vision, though not with cognitive abilities such as thinking and reasoning, we can use knowledge about the structure of the visual system and the physics of light to say what the input is. There is not room here to go into details, but basically the retina is a huge array of cells that provides information about how much light and of what colour is falling on each of its parts. Its layout, of course, corresponds to the layout of the *visual field*, which is why we see an image through an ophthalmoscope. This fact is, in turn, explained by the 'optics of the eye' – the way that the lens at the front forms an image on the retina at the back.

An information processing account says, of course, that information gets processed. So, to set up an information processing theory of vision we need to know not just what information the system has to work on, but also what information the system is trying to extract. In fact, there is no general answer to the question: what do visual systems do? The eyes of many lower animals are highly specialised. What those animals see is linked to specific needs that they have. Our own needs are more diverse, and the human visual system provides information that we can use to guide ourselves around the world in our attempts to fulfil our goals. So, from information about how much light of what colour is coming in which directions towards our two eyes, we derive information about the three-dimensional structure of our environment and the identities of the objects in it.

Here we learn another important lesson about cognitive science. Information can be processed very quickly and without our knowing what is happening. We can see why the processing of visual information must be rapid. Animals must react quickly to changes in their environment, otherwise they may perish. But all they need be aware of is the *result* of the information processing – that a lion has just come into view – not how it happens. However, this lack of awareness of the intermediate stages of information processing has an important consequence for cognitive science. *Introspective evidence cannot tell us how visual information is processed.* We need to use other, less direct, techniques in our studies.

Finally, much of the information used to make sense of a current input does not come from the input itself, but is stored in the mind. As we will see in the next chapter, for example, the processes used to analyse visual inputs have assumptions built into them about what the world is like. Or, to take another example, when we look at a pattern of black marks on a white background and see a word, we are using stored information about what words there are in English. Think of the difference between this case and looking at a word in a language (or even a script) that you do not know.

EXPLANATION, PREDICTION AND CONTROL

People become dissatisfied with everyday explanations. They may not work, or they may not apply to some phenomena. One response is to develop other kinds of explanation. Often the explanation merely gives a point to something that seems bad, such as crop failure, over which people have little control. Scientific explanations differ from other types of explanation in the potential they provide for prediction and control. This potential is reflected in the way science has changed our lives. The impact of science has been very different from that of other explanatory frameworks, mythological ones for example. Science is responsible for public health measures (via an understanding of what causes diseases and what prevents them), household electrical goods, modern weapons and a host of other innovations that deeply affect our lives, whether we understand the science on which they are based or not.

What might the consequences of cognitive science be? Because science gives the ability to control, some people feel that cognitive science is likely to be a bad thing. They fear it will enable some people to gain control over others. I believe that this fear is ill-founded. In many cases, such as the study of vision, cognitive science is unlikely to result in the ability to control other people, but rather in the ability to control defects in our visual systems (in so far as they cannot already be controlled by spectacles, contact lenses and the like). In other cases cognitive science should help people to realise when they are being manipulated, since manipulation usually depends on its victims not knowing what is happening to them. Furthermore, the more we know about our cognitive systems, and those of other people, the easier it will be to see why and how people might misunderstand each other.

THE METHODS OF COGNITIVE SCIENCE

Cognitive science is a science. That much is obvious from its name. But what does that tell us about its methods of studying cognition? Although philosophers of science have often sought to discover *the* scientific method, they have failed. Indeed, if scientific method could be captured in a formula, science would be easy, but it would be less interesting.

Perhaps the most important aspect of scientific method is that scientific questions are regarded as *empirical* questions – questions that cannot be answered by appealing to prejudice or intuition, but only by an objective examination of the facts. A corollary of this view is that scientific hypotheses are always tentative. They may be overthrown by new evidence that is incompatible with them.

Cognitive science is difficult because we all make an enormous number of assumptions about human cognition. These assumptions have a variety of sources, but most of them come either from our own experience or from folk psychology. Although these assumptions are (at least sometimes!) based on empirical evidence, as cognitive scientists we must be prepared to reject them if they are incompatible with the results of our studies. Any piece of evidence is compatible with many general statements. So, perhaps we made the wrong generalisation. Nevertheless, it can be difficult to reject ideas that we believe are supported by our experience. As cognitive scientists we must be aware that our prejudices might bias our science.

What are the methods of cognitive science? As in any other science, they are highly varied. In other sciences, physics for example, there is a division of labour between theoreticians and experimentalists. Theorists generate potential explanations of phenomena; experimentalists try to discover whether those explanations are correct. In the subdisciplines of cognitive science – of which psychology, linguistics and artificial intelligence are arguably the most important – there has been no clear distinction between theoreticians and experimentalists. In psychology, experimental work has been overemphasised, with a consequent lack of sophistication in its theories, whereas in linguistics and AI, theoreticians tend to think that the empirical data is so obvious that they do not need anyone to collect it for them. Nevertheless, a distinction can, and should, be made between constructing theories about cognitive abilities and testing their predictions.

I will illustrate the differences between the approaches of the three main subdisciplines of cognitive science by briefly presenting research on a single topic from each of the disciplines, pronouns such as *he, she, it* and *they*. I am being deliberately vague in describing the topic since, as we shall see, the three disciplines ask very different questions about pronouns.

Cognitive psychology

It is difficult to define psychology concisely. The subtitle George Miller chose for his book on psychology, 'the science of mental life', is one possible definition. Another is 'the study of experience and behaviour'. I will illustrate how cognitive psychologists try to explain cognitive abilities using one of my own experiments. The experiment was designed to answer some particular questions about how pronouns are understood.

Sometimes it is obvious who a pronoun refers to because, say, the pronoun is *he* and only one male person has been mentioned:

Max confessed to Beth because he wanted a reduced sentence.

However, in:

Max confessed to Bill because he wanted a reduced sentence

he still refers to Max, but this time we only know this because we know that confessing is one way of getting a reduced sentence. To put this point another way, we have to use our knowledge about the world to work out who did what in this sentence. We usually do not realise what is happening, of course; we understand the sentence without any problems. Or do we?

In the experiment the sentences appeared on a computer screen and subjects pressed a button as soon as they had understood them. When they pressed the button a question appeared and they had to answer 'yes' or 'no'. What I found was that when the gender of the pronoun determined who it referred to (Max and not Beth) the sentences were read more quickly than when it did not. (The questions were answered as accurately in both cases.) The experiment suggests that matching a pronoun to a person via gender is a quicker mental process than using knowledge about the world to work out who did what.

There are a number of points to note about this study. First, the two kinds of sentence are as similar as they can be. So, for example, we do not have to worry about how the words are identified, or how the sentences are related to previous context (there never is any). Second, the experiment used many subjects (16) and many pairs of sentences (32). Third, as is typical in psychological studies, the theory that the experiment tests is rather vaguely formulated. Nevertheless, our goal is a well-specified account of the mental processes that underlie the understanding of pronouns in ordinary reading.

Linguistics

Linguistics is the study of languages and what they have in common. On one view, this study is completely separate from the study of how people use languages. Its goal is to describe languages as elegantly as possible – it is a branch of applied mathematics! However, many contemporary linguists follow the doctrine of Noam Chomsky, the man primarily responsible for the growth of a scientific approach to linguistics in the past 30 years. Chomsky claims that the description of a language, which he calls a grammar, is also a description of what a *native speaker* of that language 'knows' about the language. I have put the word *knows* in scare quotes, because native speakers cannot tell you everything they 'know' about their language in this sense. Most of their knowledge is merely manifest in their use of the language. On this view, a grammar – a description of a language – is also a description of the store of information that people have in their minds, and which they use both to understand and to produce sentences.

Linguistic studies of pronouns have become highly technical in recent years. The kind of question that linguists ask about pronouns is: under what conditions can a pronoun refer to the same thing as some other expression? So, under normal circumstances *he* cannot refer to Beth. But why can *he* not refer to Bill in the following sentence?

He came into the room, after Bill dropped the plates.

Is it because *he* comes before *Bill?* No, because you can say:

After he came into the room, Bill dropped the plates.

Is it because *he* is in the main part of the sentence and *Bill* is in a so-called subordinate clause? No, because you can say:

After Bill came into the room, he dropped the plates.

Apparently, the restriction is that *Bill* cannot both come after *he* and be in a subordinate clause. Linguists have formalised this notion in terms of the way they believe that sentences are structured. We will have more to say about sentence structure in chapter 4. Let us just note one further complication. Originally, linguists believed there was a restriction only on *backwards pronominalisation*, where the pronoun comes before (i.e. backwards in the sentence from) the expression whose meaning it shares. However, there are some restrictions, even when the pronoun follows the other expression. So, in:

Near Bill, he saw a snake.

he cannot be Bill, but in:
 Near him, Bill saw a snake.
him can.

 In Chomsky's view, although people who are not professional linguists cannot state what they 'know' about English pronouns, their knowledge is reflected in their ability to use pronouns correctly. Linguists themselves use this ability, their 'intuitions' about their native language as Chomsky puts it, to provide data about the correct use of pronouns. The theories they develop to explain these data can be highly complex and technical, as is the case in theories of pronouns, although this brief account has not brought out that fact.

Artificial intelligence

Practitioners of artificial intelligence, usually referred to as AI, try to make computers do things that are regarded as marks of intelligence in people. AI can contribute to cognitive science either by identifying general principles that characterise intelligence or by producing detailed models of people's cognitive abilities. AI research usually takes the form of writing computer programs. For example, Terry Winograd wrote a program, which he called SHRDLU (well, everyone else was giving their programs *sensible* names), that took part in conversations with its user about a miniature world called BLOCKSWORLD. BLOCKSWORLD comprised a set of coloured blocks on a table top. The program should have been connected to a robot arm that could move the blocks, but the arm did not materialise, so SHRDLU had to be content with a simulation of the BLOCKSWORLD inside the computer. The following is part of a conversation with SHRDLU. Figure 1.2 shows the BLOCKSWORLD at the beginning of the conversation.

User:	Pick up a big red block.
SHRDLU:	OK.
User:	Grasp the pyramid.
SHRDLU:	I don't understand which pyramid you mean.
User:	Find a block which is taller than *the one* you are holding and put *it* into the box.
SHRDLU:	By '*it*', I assume you mean the block which is taller than *the one* I am holding.
User:	What does the box contain?
SHRDLU:	The blue pyramid and the blue block.
User:	What is the pyramid supported by?
SHRDLU:	The box.
User:	How many blocks are not in the box?
SHRDLU:	Four of *them*.

User:	Is at least *one of them* narrower than *the one* which I told you to pick up?
SHRDLU:	Yes, the red cube.
User:	Is *it* supported?
SHRDLU:	Yes, by the table.

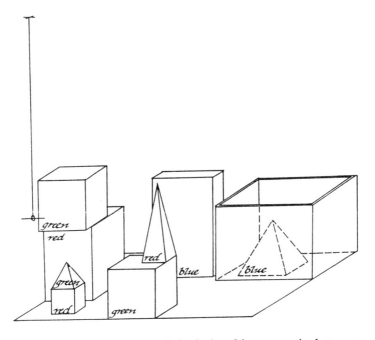

Figure 1.2 The BLOCKSWORLD at the beginning of the conversation between SHRDLU and its user

The italicised expressions, which are not italicised in the original conversation, contain either indefinite (*one*) or third person definite (*it*, *them*) pronouns. SHRDLU's apparently effortless use and understanding of these pronouns belie considerable complexities in the parts of the program that have to decide what these expressions refer to – parts of the program that might model people's ability to use pronouns.

Connectionism

To complete our discussion of the methods of cognitive science, and in particular those that use computers to model cognitive abilities, we must

OUTPUT UNITS

HIDDEN
UNITS

INPUT UNITS

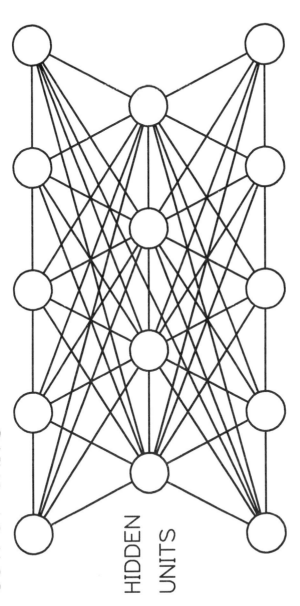

Figure 1.3 Schematic diagram of a connectionist machine. The circles represent the processing units, and the lines, the connections along which activation passes from one unit to another. Activation in one unit may either increase or decrease the activation in another unit that it is connected to, depending on whether the connection is positive (facilitatory) or negative (inhibitory)

mention a recent development – *connectionism*. Connectionism has been seen as a rival to traditional AI, of which SHRDLU is a prime example. The traditional approach assumes that what is important about cognition can be described at an abstract level, independent of the machinery – be it a brain or a computer – that underlies it. To relate this idea to a previous one, cognition should be described as the *processing of information*. And because information can be encoded in many different physical forms (e.g. printed in books, or recorded on tapes), it does not matter whether it is stored and manipulated by the electrical and chemical activity of the brain or by the on/off states of transistors in a computer. So, computers that bear no physical resemblance to brains can be programmed to simulate cognitive abilities.

When computers were first invented, a different idea about how they might help us to understand the brain gained brief popularity. The idea was to develop an abstract model of a brain cell and to use a computer to find out how a large network of such cells would work together. Since the brain itself is a network of cells, this way of using computers should show how the brain produces intelligent behaviour. This programme of research quickly ran into apparently insuperable problems, but recently some of these problems have been solved and a new range of neural network models, the so-called connectionist models, has been developed. There are, as yet, no connectionist models of text comprehension. Indeed there is some doubt about whether there will ever be. So, I cannot show how a connectionist machine would deal with pronouns.

A connectionist machine comprises a number, often a very large number, of simple interconnected units (hence the name 'connectionism'). The units pass activation to one another, with the activation of each unit being fixed by the amounts of positive and negative activation reaching it. One set of units are *input units*. These units are activated by something outside the network, and patterns of activation in them represent features of what the model is processing. This method of encoding an input can be compared, for example, to the way that a pattern of activity in the cells in the retina of the eye encodes information about the scene that the eye is looking at. Another set of units are *output units*. The pattern of activation in these units indicates the machine's response to its input. Many different types of response are possible. For example, a connection machine may classify its input by having two output units, with high activation of one standing for 'yes' (it is a dog, or whatever) and of the other for 'no' (it isn't). In a more complex example the pattern of activation of input units encodes the spelling of a word and that in the output units encodes the way the word sounds. Between the input units and the output units there may be one or more other layers of units, which are called *hidden units*, and which considerably increase the capabilities of connectionist machines.

Connectionism is a controversial topic. Its proponents claim that its brain-style modelling is more realistic than that of traditional AI. They also argue that it explains aspects of cognition that traditional AI models have difficulty with. For example, such models are often unable to process inputs that are slightly degraded, sentences with minor grammatical errors, for instance, or views of objects through windows with raindrops running down them. Connectionist models would produce a slightly weaker output, but one that was still basically correct. Connectionism's detractors argue that connectionist models cannot adequately cope with the complex rule-governed information processing that characterises much of cognition, particularly language and reasoning. Connectionist models can only relate things by the unstructured relation of *association* (one thing often goes with another). And, the anti-connectionists argue, although associationism is a theory of mind that has been put forward several times in the past, by empiricist philosophers from John Locke onwards, and by behaviourist psychologists such as Watson and Skinner, there are insuperable objections to it.

MECHANICAL METAPHORS AND REDUCTIONISM

The fact that all explanations, including scientific ones, come to an end with principles, which have to be accepted without explanation for the time being, raises a further question: what sorts of principles will the explanations of cognitive science rest on? Behind this question lurks the spectre of 'reductionism' – the idea that psychological explanations can be replaced by explanations in terms of brain functioning or even in terms of physics and chemistry. Some people find this idea 'dehumanising', others are quite happy with it.

It's a commonplace in the philosophy of science that one science can only be reduced to another, more basic, one in an in-principle sense. Take evolutionary biology, for example. Breakthroughs in biochemistry, in the 1950s and after, have uncovered in increasing detail the mechanisms by which offspring inherit characteristics from their parents. We can see how, in principle, the theory of evolution fits together with a biochemical account of inheritance. But a scientific theory of evolution still needs concepts such as gene pool and evolutionary stable strategy, which cannot be defined in biochemical terms. Similarly, although a scientific approach to cognition assumes that perceiving and thinking depend on brain functioning, there will always be a need for a level of explanation in which cognitive concepts play a role. Cognitive science will no more be replaced by physiology than the theory of evolution has been replaced by biochemistry.

Some people worry that cognitive science is dehumanising because its explanations of cognitive functioning assume that people are machines or, at least, that they have important similarities with machines. This machine metaphor is difficult to assess because there are two different concepts of machine. The everyday concept has as its central examples simple mechanical devices. No one claims that minds are like that kind of machine. However, a more recent concept of a machine is one in which computers have a central place. This idea of a machine is in turn derived from a more abstract, technical, concept developed by the mathematician and Second World War codebreaker Alan Turing. A Turing 'machine' is not a machine at all in the everyday sense. It is a mathematical abstraction that has the following property: if something can be worked out by mathematical calculation, in the broadest sense of that term, there is a Turing machine that can work it out. Indeed, not only is there a Turing machine that can do each specific calculation, there is a General Turing machine that can do all of them. The way it works is that you pick the calculation you want done and tell the General Turing machine about the ordinary Turing machine that does that calculation. The General Turing machine then simulates the operation of the more specific one.

A modern computer can be thought of as a concrete realisation of the General Turing machine. You pick a calculation, and load a program for doing that calculation into the computer's memory. The program corresponds to a description of a specific Turing machine for doing that calculation. The computer can then simulate what would happen if you had that special machine.

One further observation will make the point of this discussion clear. The word 'calculation' is used in a general sense in which it covers all the mathematical operations of modern maths. These operations are not restricted to addition, subtraction, multiplication and division, but include transformations that might describe, say, the processing of information in the visual system or the language understanding system.

The relevance of Turing machines to cognitive science should now be clear. If we use mathematics, of whatever kind, to describe cognitive information processing, our cognitive systems will correspond to Turing machines, in the sense that for each such cognitive system, there will be a Turing machine that does the same calculations as the cognitive system. In this qualified sense, cognitive science is committed to the idea that the mind is a 'machine'.

We have still to show that mechanistic metaphors for the mind are not dehumanising. I hope that this book will help to do so by sketching models of cognitive processes that do justice to the complexity and subtlety of those processes. What I cannot hope to do, however, is to solve the so-called problem of free will, which has exercised philosophers for centuries, and which is raised again by the mind as machine metaphor. If the mind is a machine, even in our attenuated Turing machine sense, its operation must be governed by the causal laws of physics. There seems to be no room in this sort of account for the freedom we feel we have in deciding what to do. It is easy to reconcile a scientific approach to cognition with the idea that people think they have free will. When someone is faced with a decision, they are aware of (at least some of) the alternative courses of action available to them. They are not, however, aware of all of the factors that influence their decision making. They think they are making a free choice, but in an obvious sense they are not. In desperation some people have appealed to quantum physics and Heisenberg's uncertainty principle to allow for freedom of the will, but most cognitive scientists believe that the principle is irrelevant. It is, therefore, difficult to see a place for genuinely free will in cognitive science.

FURTHER READING

Phil Johnson-Laird's *The Computer and the Mind* (Fontana, 1988) is a more advanced introduction to cognitive science than the present one, with an even greater emphasis on the role of computation. The first American-style undergraduate textbook on cognitive science, which provides much broader coverage than the present book, is *Cognitive Science: An Introduction* by Stillings, Feinstein, Garfield, Rissland, Rosenbaum, Weisler and Baker-Ward (MIT Press, 1987). *Foundations of Cognitive Science*, edited by Michael Posner (MIT Press, 1989) is more detailed and more advanced still. My own *Artificial Intelligence: An Introduction* (Routledge, 1988) provides an introduction to that subject.

2 The senses

Seeing, hearing, smelling, tasting, touching and sensing the position of our bodies – almost all of us can take these sensory abilities for granted. Certainly we do not have to worry about how our senses work when we use them. Indeed, there are many situations in which it could be dangerous to stop and think about how our senses work. If you see a stone flying towards your head, you do not stop to think how you managed to recognise it, you get out of the way quickly, if you can. Nevertheless, we all know of or about people who have lost, or never had, one or more of their senses. And particularly with the blind and the deaf we realise something of the impact their deficits must have on their lives. Thinking about the experience of blind and deaf people can also suggest answers to the question of what our senses are for.

For people, sight is the most important sense, though for many other animals it is not. Sight is also the best understood of our senses. For this reason this chapter will focus on vision. We will also discuss hearing to some extent, but the other senses will be mentioned only briefly at the end of the chapter.

VISION

If a sighted person closes their eyes and tries to move around, even in a very familiar space, they find it difficult. If they cannot see something they find it difficult to know exactly where it is and to avoid bumping into it. Although it would be a gross insult to the blind to suggest that closing one's eyes gives a good idea of what it is like to be blind, especially congenitally blind, it does show that one of the major functions of vision is to tell us what is where, so that we can move around our environment safely and efficiently.

So much might seem obvious, but only recently have cognitive scientists faced the challenge of describing how the visual system is able to provide this information. There have been two major reasons for this tardiness. First, simple though the formulation of the problem is, it is a difficult one to solve.

Second, partly because this general problem is so difficult, the study of vision has focused on easier topics. In particular, psychologists and physiologists have sought to explain such phenomena as visual illusions, the detection of motion, and the way we perceive colours. The physiological side of this work has become highly technical. It has led, for example in the field of colour vision, to detailed explanations of why any coloured light can be matched by a mixture of just three other colours, and of why colour blindness and anomalous colour vision, which are common particularly in men, take the forms they do. However, until comparatively recently, psychological work on vision has tended to identify a plurality of interesting effects (a large number of visual illusions, for example) all in search of an explanation.

In the last twenty years the work of David Marr and his colleagues, at the Massachusetts Institute of Technology (in Cambridge, Massachusetts), has transformed the study of vision. Before his untimely death, Marr brought together ideas from psychology, neurophysiology and artificial intelligence in a new approach to the study of vision. He stated clearly, perhaps for the first time, the goal of a theory of visual processing, at least for man and other higher mammals. That goal is to explain how the visual system 'build[s] a description of the shapes and positions of *things* from *images*' (emphases added). In this statement Marr recognises that the input to the visual system is an image. Indeed, as we saw in chapter 1, it is an uninterpreted image. Information enters the visual system when light from a source such as the sun or an electric light is reflected from objects on which it falls into the human eye. Initially, that light is absorbed by *receptor cells* in the retina, which respond in a way that depends, not quite straightforwardly, on the amount of light falling on them. The receptor cells in the retina have two other important properties. First, the way they are set out corresponds to the spatial layout of the visual field, in roughly the same way that each point on a photographic negative corresponds to a particular part of the scene that the camera is pointed at. Most importantly, neighbouring points on the retina correspond to neighbouring directions in space. In photography the result is a picture that our visual systems can interpret as a scene. In the human visual system the result is that subsequent information processing stages of the visual system can assume that the information they receive is spatially organised.

The second important property of the receptor cells is that they come in four types. Those called *rods*, which are insensitive to colour, are by far the most common. Indeed, the perception of colour plays a comparatively small role in the processes that interested Marr, and in most of his work he was able to ignore colour vision. Similarly, although black and white photos, films and TV programmes have a different feel from those in colour, it is hardly more difficult to recognise the objects in them. The other three types of receptor cell are called *cones* and are responsible for our seeing in colour and for the sharpness with which we see what we are looking at directly.

How does the visual system identify objects from images? Marr identified three main stages in the process. In the first, the visual system starts with a *grey-level description* of the image. For each point in the visual field, the grey-level description encodes the intensity of light coming from the corresponding direction in space. This information is provided by the receptor cells in the retina, again ignoring colour. The primary purpose of this first stage of visual processing, according to Marr, is to discover regions in the image and their boundaries. There are two things to note here. First, this initial stage of processing converts one image into another – regions and boundaries are parts of images, not parts of things in the world. Second, it is no good saying that boundaries can easily be recognised in images because they occur at the edges of objects. The point of this initial stage of image processing is to move closer to the point where objects can be identified. But none has been, so we cannot use the objects to recognise the boundaries! The boundaries must be identified in terms of properties of the image.

Nevertheless, one might think, it is easy to detect boundary lines in an image and to divide it into regions. Unfortunately it is not, for the following reason. A boundary is a place in the image where there is a *relatively* sharp transition from light to dark (remember, we are ignoring colour). We are forced to say a relatively sharp transition, because transitions in real images are not absolutely clear. But now we are faced with the problem: what counts as relatively sharp? To take just one example, if a surface is lit from the side, its image changes from lighter (in the part of the image corresponding to the part of the object nearest to the light) to darker. We cannot identify every transition from light to dark as a boundary, or we will conclude that the whole image is made up of boundaries.

This problem in finding boundaries is made more acute by an assumption made by Marr, which reflects what is known about the anatomy of the visual system. Marr assumed that transitions from light to dark are discovered by *local computations*. Such computations compare the intensity at one point in the image only with that at points near to it. Anatomically, only neighbouring receptor cells are connected together by cells in the next layer of the visual system (these cells are actually still in the retina). A global computation could identify intensity changes across a large area of an image, ones caused by lighting for example, and discount them. A local computation, unless it is a sophisticated one of the kind Marr proposed, might confuse lighting effects with blurred or not very distinct edges.

How did Marr solve this problem? He proposed that the visual system performs not one set of local computations but several (four, in one of his computer models). Each set of computations works on a different scale. The

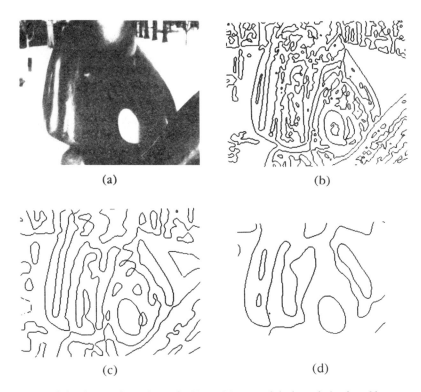

Figure 2.1 Picture of a sculpture by Henry Moore and the boundaries found by sets of detectors operating at three scales. The detectors working at the smallest scale are the ones that find most detail in the image

first looks for very local changes in intensity. It can detect very fine detail, but it is also sensitive to changes in intensity that do not correspond to edges of objects. The other computations work on increasingly larger scales. Again, this idea fits with what is known about the visual system. Some receptor cells have very small *receptive fields* – they respond only to light in a very small area of the visual field. Others have larger receptive fields. A receptor cell cannot tell where in its receptive field light is falling. So, if cells with large receptive fields are used to detect changes in intensity, they will not be very accurate at detecting where those changes in intensity occur. To illustrate these ideas, a picture of a sculpture by Henry Moore, and the boundaries detected in it by computations at three different scales, are shown in figure 2.1. Marr's trick was to combine information from the different sets of computations. For example, if a change in intensity detected by cells with large receptive fields lies at the same place in the image as one detected by the cells with small receptive fields, it probably corresponds to the edge of an object. If it does not, it is probably best explained as an effect of lighting. Using this kind of argument, a start can be made in distinguishing properties of the image that depend on the objects in the scene from those that depend on other factors.

Marr called the new representation derived from the grey-level description of the image, and containing information about edges and the regions they enclose, the *primal sketch*. The way the primal sketch is derived from the grey-level description is too complicated to detail here. The detection of changes in intensity can be described using relatively straightforward mathematics, though it is daunting for those who are not mathematically minded. The rules for combining information from the cells with different sizes of receptive field are complicated because they must take account of peculiar effects that arise in certain lighting conditions.

The main purpose in converting a grey-level description into a primal sketch is to get a more useful, less cluttered, description of the image – hence the term *sketch*. The next major stage in visual processing, according to Marr, is the conversion of the primal sketch into a *2½-D sketch*. The 2½-D sketch is no longer an image. It contains information about the surfaces *in the world* that produce the image, and about their relative orientations. It therefore contains 3-D information. Marr called it the 2½-D sketch because one of the three dimensions is incompletely represented. Information about the absolute distance of the surfaces from the viewer is inaccurate, even though that about relative distances of different surfaces is not.

No objects have yet been identified, so surfaces cannot be identified in terms of the objects of which they are part. How, then, is the 2½-D sketch constructed? Marr's answer is that a variety of computations are performed on the information in the primal sketch. These computations are performed independently and their results are combined in the 2½-D sketch, which acts as a very short-term memory while the computations are carried out. What are these computations? The three that have been studied in most detail are: *stereopsis, structure from motion* and *shape from shading*.

Most people are familiar with the phenomenon of stereopsis. Our two eyes have slightly different views of the world, as is obvious when we open and close them separately. Because the eyes turn inwards, the image of the object that a person is focusing on lies at the same point on the two retinas. The images of other objects, however, would be displaced to a greater or lesser extent relative to one another if the images on the two retinas were superimposed. The different displacements are straightforwardly related to the distance of the objects from the one in focus. Those distances can, therefore, be computed from the differences between the two images. A stereoscope fools the eyes into seeing depth by presenting separate, slightly different, pictures to the two eyes. In one kind of stereoscope spectacles with one green and one red lens are worn, and red and green pictures are printed on the page. The red lens filters out the red image, so its eye sees only the green image, and vice versa. Another type uses magnifying lenses or a dividing panel to force each eye to look at a different picture. Another uses polaroid lenses to present light polarised in different planes to the two eyes. Stereo movies use similar techniques to present a sequence of stereo images.

Most demonstrations of stereopsis use line drawings or photos in which the objects can easily be identified. Indeed, one might ask, how can the difference between the images in the two eyes be measured, if the objects cannot be identified? The answer is by comparing the grey-level descriptions. This phenomenon is illustrated by the existence of so-called *random-dot stereograms*. To create a random-dot stereogram one takes a random pattern of black and white dots, and creates another very similar one by shifting a central area, getting rid of the dots that part of it covers, and filling in the blank patch with more random dots. The original pattern is then presented to one eye and the derived pattern to the other. On its own each pattern looks flat. Viewed stereoscopically, the shifted portion appears to float above or below the rest (see figure 2.2).

The relevance of random-dot stereograms to Marr's theory is that they demonstrate the stereoscopic identification of surfaces at different depths *before any objects have been recognised*. Marr's contribution was to show how, by making certain assumptions about what the world is like, a stereoscopic *depth map* can be produced from information about the images in the two eyes – information that is in the primal sketch, but which does not identify the objects in the scene. Marr's assumptions are all general ones, and they play a crucial role in his theory. One example is the assumption that continuous surfaces make up a much greater proportion of the visual field than boundaries. So if what you see looks like a continuous surface it almost certainly is one (rather than, say, two different surfaces at different distances cleverly lit to make it look as if they were the same surface).

The computation of structure from motion is related to the observation that moving objects are easier to see than ones that are still. That is why stick insects, for example, are safer from predators if they remain motionless. If something in the distance moves, we may be able to say little more than that some object or other moved. However, the movement of closer objects, particularly those that have been camouflaged in some way, often helps us to see their shape. This fact is demonstrated by another 'random dot' demonstration – the *random-dot movie*. Consider an object with spots all over its surface. Take a film of it in motion so that only the spots are visible. Now

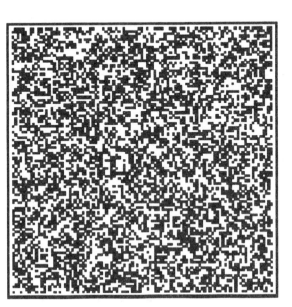

Figure 2.2 A random dot stereogram. Some readers may be able to see the stereogram in depth by focusing their eyes either well behind or well in front of the page. Focusing in front of the page may be helped by placing a finger tip in front of the page and staring at it. Both techniques are designed to ensure that the two halves of the stereogram are seen (primarily) by different eyes

look at a single frame of the film. If the dots are thinly scattered, it will not be possible to see what the object is. However, when the film is run, the shape of the object will be seen.

In a random-dot stereogram, two images separated in space, in neither of which a surface can be seen, are combined by the visual system to produce an effect of depth. In a random-dot movie, images separated in time are combined with similar results. Shimon Ullman, a student of Marr's, showed how the visual system might work out the shape of an object from the way parts of its image move relative to one another over time – he showed how 'structure from motion' could be computed from the primal sketch and encoded in the 2½-D sketch. Again, the computations make use of general assumptions about what the world is like. And, like the computations that derive stereoscopic depth, Ullman's structure from motion computations are local in the sense described above.

The idea behind shape from shading, our third computation contributing to the 2½-D sketch, is again straightforward. In pencil or pen-and-ink sketches (in the artistic sense!) shading techniques can produce an impression of depth in a 2-D image. These techniques depend on the fact that some parts of 3-D objects may cast shadows and others may be hidden from light sources. The shading around an object depends on three principal factors: its shape, the nature of its surfaces (e.g. shiny or matt), and the source or sources of light. There is no 'random dot' demonstration for shape from shading. The nearest equivalent is that objects can be depicted without contours, simply by shading. And, as we have seen before, if the visual system uses shading to *identify* surfaces, it must be able to do so without knowing what objects it is looking at. The shading itself, together with the general assumptions that are always important in Marr's theories, must be sufficient to determine what the surfaces are.

The difficult part of the shape from shading problem is to separate the contributions of the three factors – the shape of the surfaces, the light-reflecting properties of the surfaces and the lighting – to the pattern of light and dark in the image. No general solution to the problem has been discovered, as it has for stereopsis and structure from motion. There are only solutions for special cases: in particular, one for matt objects illuminated by a distant 'point' source of light. It is possible that shading does not make such an important contribution to the 2½-D sketch as stereopsis and structure from motion. However, Marr himself argued that the ability of make-up, particularly in the theatre, to create an impression of depth that other cues cannot, shows that its contribution to human visual processing should not be ignored.

The three processes of stereopsis, structure from motion and shape from shading, together with others such as shape from optical flow and orientation from surface contours, contribute information to the 2½-D sketch and thus

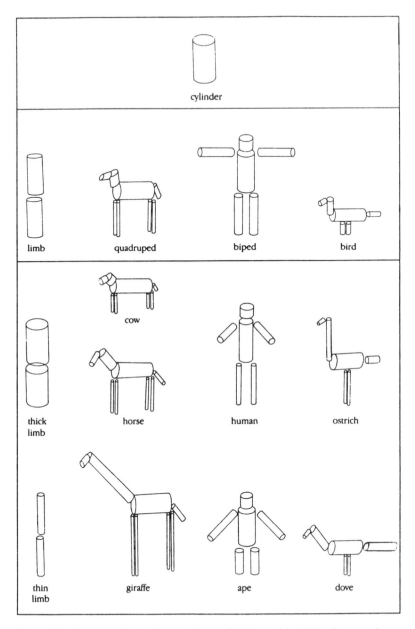

Figure 2.3 Some entries in the catalogue of 3-D models. This diagram shows simplified models made up of ordinary cylinders, rather than generalised cylinders. It also indicates how the catalogue might be organised

to the identification of the surfaces that a person is looking at and their orientations. One of Marr's more controversial claims is that it is not only possible to analyse stereo-depth, structure from motion and shading without knowing what objects are present, but that the human visual system *always* works that way. In the jargon of cognitive science, Marr believed the construction of the 2½-D sketch to be a *data-driven* process that depends only on the image (together with general assumptions about what images are usually like), not on hypotheses about what objects are depicted in a particular image.

The final stage of visual processing, according to Marr, is the construction of a *3-D model description* from the 2½-D sketch. The 3-D model description contains information about the identity and 3-D structure of the objects in the scene. In many ways this final stage of visual processing is the most difficult to describe. Marr's account is highly speculative, and less closely tied to the psychological and neurophysiological facts than his theories of lower-level visual processing.

The identity of objects in a scene can only be established using stored information about what objects look like. However, Marr argued that, in many cases though not all, 3-D structure can be derived from the 2½-D sketch using only general principles of the kind he used in his theory of lower-level vision. Marr's basic insight again rests on a simple observation – stick figure representations, particularly of such things as animals and plants, are easy to recognise. But how are stick figures related to the ordinary people, animals and plants we usually see? Marr argued that people's bodies, for example, can be represented as jointed cylinders, or, more realistically, as *generalised cylinders* that change their size along their length. He then showed that the cylinders an object is made up of can be computed from the 2½-D sketch. The lines running down the centre of these cylinders, which are important in the recognition process, make up stick figures.

Once a generalised cylinder representation of the objects in a scene has been computed, it can be compared with stored representations of objects in a *catalogue of 3-D models*. Simplified versions of some of the entries in this catalogue are shown in figure 2.3. In the catalogue the objects are represented in 'standard' orientations. To match them against a representation of a scene they will usually need to be rotated and to have their joints bent. These processes do not present any problems in principle, but matching may be difficult in practice – when there is gross foreshortening in the image for example. Marr envisaged a process of progressive refinement of the interpretation of parts of scenes. Once the best-fitting model has been selected from the catalogue, it suggests interpretations for parts of the image that are unclear or obscured – an arm partly hidden behind a doorpost, or whatever.

Marr's account of this final stage of visual processing is more controversial than his account of the earlier stages. He tried to make his account as general as possible, but there are many things, for example screwed up pieces of paper, that cannot usefully be analysed into generalised cylinders. Marr specifically contrasted his ideas with earlier work on object recognition in artificial intelligence. This work was based on an assumption common in AI in the late 1960s and early 1970s. This assumption was that difficult problems, such as object recognition, should be studied in miniature worlds, where the problem was easier to solve, and that the solution should be generalised to more difficult cases in the real world. A particularly popular miniature world was the MIT BLOCKSWORLD (see chapter 1), which comprised a set of prismatic solids (cubes, pyramids) on a table top. For scene analysis programs BLOCKSWORLD contained matt white blocks set against a black background.

A number of *line finding* programs analysed images of BLOCKSWORLD scenes produced by a TV camera. Some were bottom-up analysers, working from information in the image itself, and general properties of BLOCKS-WORLD scenes. Others guessed what objects were in the scene on the basis of a preliminary analysis and then worked top-down, looking for lines undetected in the preliminary analysis but which should be there if the scene really contained those objects.

Line finding programs use a rudimentary, and less general, version of Marr's technique for finding boundaries in an image – one aspect of computing a primal sketch. However, most BLOCKSWORLD vision programs focused on a different problem, the *segmentation problem*. Indeed, many later programs had line drawings as their input – the problem of line finding was solved for them. To solve the segmentation problem is to decide which surfaces in a BLOCKSWORLD scene are part of the same object. A solution to this problem segments the image into parts that belong to the same object, though it does not identify the objects. The nature of the problem is indicated in figure 2.4.

Two main techniques were developed for solving the segmentation problem in the BLOCKSWORLD. One depends on distinguishing things in the image (lines and junctions between lines) from things in the scene (edges and vertices), and developing an explicit scheme for inferring properties of the scene from properties of the image. In simple images (of scenes with no shadows and in which no more than three lines meet at any point) there are three kinds of line (which correspond to boundaries, inside edges and outside edges in the scene) and four basic types of line junction (Ts, Ys, Ls and →s). When impossible junctions have been excluded, the three line types and four junction types allow a total of 16 types of junction, which correspond to different types of vertex in the scene. These types of junction are illustrated

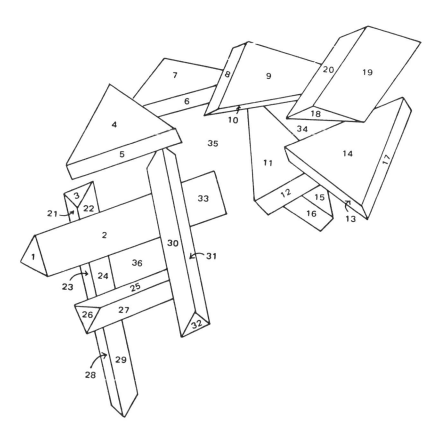

Figure 2.4 A BLOCKSWORLD scene that is comparatively difficult to segment. Many of the blocks are partly hidden behind others (e.g. the one with surfaces 3, 21, 22, 23, 24, 28, 29). The block with surfaces 6 and 7 is particularly difficult to identify, as it has no visible vertices that are useful to the segmentation process

in figure 2.5. Junctions can be labelled directly as Ts, Ys, Ls and →s, but the lines cannot be directly labelled. However, the set of derived junction types, together with one general constraint, allows most images to be segmented successfully. The general constraint is the *consistency constraint* – any line must have the same label along the whole of its length.

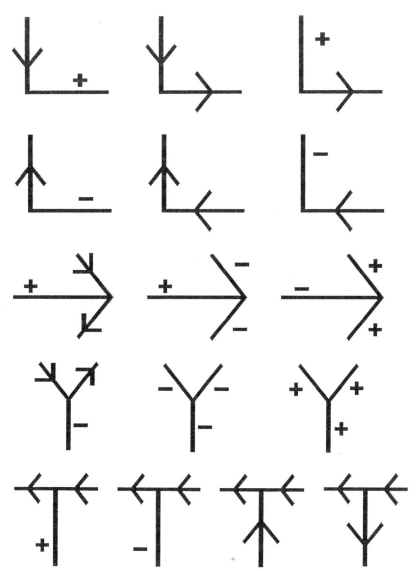

Figure 2.5 The sixteen derived junction types for scenes made up of simple blocks without edges or cracks. No more than three lines meet at any point in the image of such a scene. The three types of line are represented as follows: a plus sign indicates an outside (convex) edge, a minus sign indicates an inside (concave) edge, an arrow indicates a boundary (occluding edge). For convex and concave edges, one face of the block lies on each side of the line. For boundaries, both faces lie to the right, if one is moving in the direction of the arrow, and one of them is hidden from view

David Waltz extended this work in two ways. First, he showed how to interpret junctions at which more than three lines meet. Second, he considered images of blocks with cracks and images with shadows. In these images some lines – cracks and edges of shadows – run across one side of a block, rather than dividing two blocks from each other. These extensions may seem comparatively minor, but they increase the number of kinds of line to 11 and, more significantly, they increase the number of legitimate derived junction types from 16 to about 2500. This increase in the number of junction types would appear to increase the number of possibilities that must be considered in labelling and then segmenting an image. However, by using general constraints more effectively, Waltz was able to segment images more quickly and to segment more images correctly.

The second technique for segmenting images makes use of information about the relative slopes of surfaces in the image. It looks for a consistent interpretation of an image in which as many lines as possible correspond to edges of objects rather than to places where one object obscures the view of one behind it. In this latter case, called occlusion, the line marks the edge of one object (the front one) but not an edge of the other one. Like the technique of using labels on line junctions, this method of segmenting images is reasonably successful, but there are some images that it fails to segment properly.

These two techniques for segmenting images gave rise to some ingenious programs for interpreting images, but in an important sense they were failures. The original idea of studying object recognition in the limited domain of the BLOCKSWORLD was to solve the problem and to generalise the solution to more realistic cases. However, although it is not immediately obvious, the two segmentation techniques are inextricably bound up with properties of the BLOCKSWORLD. This link is clearer in a more successful method for segmenting BLOCKSWORLD images, called *sidedness reasoning*, invented by Steve Draper. Sidedness reasoning is reasoning about whether two points or surfaces are on the same side or different sides of a third surface. The technique only works if the surfaces are flat, as they are in the BLOCKS-WORLD. However, the real world is not made up of prismatic solids, and images of the real world cannot, in general, be successfully interpreted using sidedness reasoning.

There is a further problem with programs that segment images: segmentation is not particularly useful as a step toward object recognition, for two reasons. First, although it is easy to say what counts as one BLOCKSWORLD object and what counts as two, in the real world it is not. Is a wing mirror part of a car, or an object in its own right? How should an image of a car be 'segmented'? Second, segmentation does not provide detailed information about the shapes of objects, but only qualitative information about how their parts are oriented relative to one another. In the BLOCKSWORLD we know that an object with six sides will be a cube, but in the real world we cannot make such an assumption.

HEARING

Hearing is not so important in providing detailed information about our surroundings as vision, though other animals rely on sounds much more than humans do. The most important use of our sense of hearing is in perceiving speech. Indeed, much of what we know about hearing has been discovered by people with an interest in speech. However, ears have not evolved to analyse language, and it is hard to characterise the purpose of hearing in the way that Marr characterised the purpose of vision as constructing a representation of the objects that surround us and their locations. Nevertheless, our auditory system produces a complex analysis of the sounds falling on our ears, one which allows us to infer where they come from and what they mean.

What are the differences between seeing and hearing? Perhaps the most obvious is that most of the things we see do *not* give out their own light, but only reflect light. Even the moon's light is reflected from the sun. Most of the things we hear produce their own sounds. Although objects reflect sound, the primary result of such reflections is to alter the quality of the sounds we hear, as for example in a concert hall. The blind do use reflected sound, for example, from the taps of their sticks, to identify what is in front of them. Furthermore, the location and recognition of objects from the way they reflect sound are highly developed in the *echolocation* systems of some species of bat. In order to see things, animals typically rely on a natural source of light, the sun, to illuminate things and make them visible. There is no corresponding natural source of sound, so bats produce their own, or rather they produce ultrasound – 'noises' too high in pitch for the human ear to perceive. By analysing the way their pulses of ultrasound are echoed, bats can navigate through a dark world and locate and catch food, mainly in the form of insects. Echolocation systems have much in common with radar and sonar.

Sounds are carried through the air (or through any other material) by the vibration of its molecules. The vibrating molecules have two effects. First, they strike the outer ear (or pinna), which provides information about the direction the sound is coming from. Second, they set in motion the air inside the ear, which hits the eardrum and sets the small bones (or ossicles) of the middle ear in motion. The purpose of the ossicles is to convert the (comparatively!) large, low energy, vibrations of the air in the outer ear into small, high energy, vibrations that are suitable for driving the apparatus of the inner ear. In particular, the vibrations are transmitted to the *basilar membrane*, which is contained in a snail-shaped fluid-filled cavity called the *cochlea*.

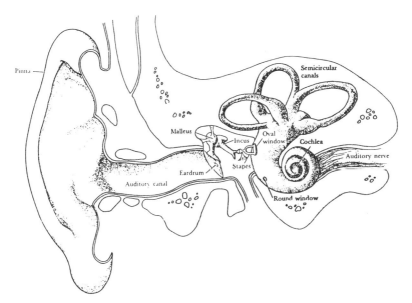

Figure 2.6 The human ear, showing the internal structures referred to in the text

Along the length of the basilar membrane lies the *organ of Corti*, which converts the mechanical vibrations of the membrane to electrical impulses in a set of nerve cells called *hair cells*, which have no connection with the hair that grows on the body's surface! These electrical impulses carry information about the sounds being heard to the brain. Figure 2.6 shows the structure of the human ear.

There is a particular type of sound called a pure tone (or sine wave). It is the kind of sound that a tuning fork makes. It has been known since the last century that any sound can be thought of as being made up from pure tones of different pitch and loudness. To take a simple example, a pure middle C has 256 vibrations per second. However, musical instruments do not produce pure tones. When middle C is played on a particular instrument it will 'contain' components with frequencies that are whole number multiples of 256. Differences between instruments depend largely on which of these *harmonics* are present, and how strong they are. Analysing a sound into pure tones is called *Fourier analysis*, after the nineteenth-century French mathematician who showed that such an analysis was always possible. The basilar membrane carries out something similar to Fourier analysis.

Bats use their echolocation systems, just as we use our sense of sight, to find out about objects in their vicinity. To some extent people can acquire this skill, as the blind do. However, people do not usually process sounds in this way and, largely for this reason, the cognitive science of hearing is different from the cognitive science of seeing. In so far as we use non-speech sounds to identify objects it is by associating a (typically very complex) sound with the kind of object that makes it. Although the sound may be complex, its structure, unlike the structure in the pattern of light that falls on the retina, does not correspond in any direct way to the structure of the object that makes it.

The processing of speech sounds, which will be discussed further in chapter 4, is different again. In language a sound with a particular structure is arbitrarily chosen as, say, the name for a particular kind of animal. A speaker of English has to learn that the name is 'dog', a speaker of Dutch, 'hond', a speaker of French, 'chien', and so on. Once a person has learned a language, what they have to do when listening to speech is to decide which of the words they know are strung together to make the utterance they are currently hearing. This identification is difficult because two instances of the same sound, two different people saying 'dog', for example, are, in physical terms, different. The basilar membrane will analyse the sounds differently. It is only at a higher level that they are classified as the same. Specifying the basis on which they are classified as the same is very difficult, though a great deal has been learned about speech sounds over the last thirty years or so.

THE OTHER SENSES

Traditional wisdom recognises three senses other than sight and hearing: taste, smell and touch. Although there are long and respectable traditions in which these senses are studied, those traditions lie within physiology and sensory psychology rather than cognitive science. Although taste and smell have cognitive components, they are similar to hearing (of non-speech sounds) in that the link between tastes and smells and the things that have them is one of association. The complexity of a taste or smell does not reflect the structure of the object that produces it, but rather its chemical nature.

The scientific study of taste defines taste as a contact sense. Taste is mediated by the taste buds, so we can only taste things that touch our tongues. The sensations produced by the taste buds are comparatively undifferentiated, a fact that seems to go against the folk psychology of taste – foods and wines can have extremely subtle flavours. But, what we call 'flavour' (or 'taste' in the everyday sense) is not detected entirely by the taste buds. The smell, texture and temperature of food all contribute to its taste in this sense. So, wine tasters are said to have good noses, not good mouths or good tongues. The taste buds respond to four principal tastes – sweet, sour, bitter and salty – though there is some disagreement about whether there might be more. The physiological basis of these four types of taste remains to be discovered.

Our sense of smell is more subtle than our sense of taste and bears primary responsibility for our enjoyment or otherwise of food and drink. Much is known about its physiology, though our ability to recognise so many different smells remains largely unexplained. Unlike taste, smell can be used to detect objects at a distance. Animals such as dogs and moles are more reliant on their sense of smell than people are. They will often locate something by following a scent – a trail of a smelly substance left by an animal or object as it moves through an environment. Other animals, some insects in particular, can follow gradients of smell, for example, to locate their mates. If an insect releases a smell into the air, the smell gets weaker as it diffuses away from the insect. If another insect detects the smell and moves in the direction in which the smell gets stronger it will eventually reach the first insect. The smells that insects release are called pheromones, and the sensitivity of pheromone-tracking insects is remarkable. Simpler organisms also track chemical gradients, though not always using what we would recognise as a sense of smell.

Touch is by definition a contact sense, which provides information about various properties of objects – temperature, roughness, size, location and weight, for example. The physiological mechanisms that detect these properties are largely separate, so what the layperson regards as a single sense of touch is more appropriately thought of as a collection of different senses. Related to these senses is another sense, or set of senses, the ability to feel pain. There have been some remarkable advances in the understanding of the physiology and biochemistry of pain in the last decade, but its cognitive science remains undeveloped.

Touch is like vision in that it can provide direct information about the shape of objects. In the case of large objects we not only have to touch them to discover their shape, we also have to move our hands around them. In doing so we are relying on a further sense, which psychologists call *proprioception*. Proprioception is knowing where the parts of our body are. It is the sense that tells us whether our arms are by our sides or up in the air even if we cannot see them. Again much is known about the physiology of touch and proprioception, but little is known about the high-level processes that enable us to recognise objects on the basis of how they feel.

FURTHER READING

John Frisby's *Seeing* (Oxford University Press, 1979) is a good introduction to the cognitive science of vision. David Marr's *Vision* (Freeman, 1982) is more difficult, but well worth the effort. Richard Dawkins provides an entertaining discussion of echolocation in bats in *The Blind Watchmaker* (Longman, 1986).

3   Memory – the storehouse of knowledge

Memories are with us all the time. Memories of people, of places and of things. Memories add texture to our lives and give us our sense of who we are. Clive Waring, the musician who has lost the ability to remember what has happened for more than a few minutes, has also suffered a great personality change. His wife described him as 'raw emotion'. Yet despite the importance of memory in our everyday lives, it is not a central research topic in cognitive science and, at least until recently, work on memory in cognitive psychology would have appeared idiosyncratic to the uninitiated.

What are the everyday facts about memory that a scientific theory should explain? Ironically, they are facts about both how bad our memories are and how good they are. In what sense are our memories bad? Even people who have good memories often cannot remember things they want to. Yet the (long-term) memory of a home computer – its disc system – can store an indefinite amount of information for an indefinite amount of time, barring accidents! And it is not that our memories are too small. Unlike a disc, they do not fill up and then refuse to store anything else. Our memories are selective, and cognitive scientists would like to explain how and why they select what they store.

In what sense are our memories good? Not just in the sense that they hold an enormous amount of information. Indeed, we find unrelated or loosely related facts hard to remember, and people like Leslie Welsh, the 'memory man' who knew so many sporting records and facts about sporting events, are regarded with amazement. What is remarkable about our memories is the speed with which we usually find the information we want. Computers can store vast amounts of information, but they rely on their users to organise it, by putting related files on the same disc for example. And the more information computers have to search through, the slower they get. Human memory allows fast access on a machine (the brain) whose basic operations are slow compared with those of computers. We do not yet understand how its organisation makes this fast access possible.

Many attempts to describe the organisation of memory fail to distinguish between an account of the *contents* of memory and an account of its organisation. For example, one programme of AI research, whose primary goal is to explain how we understand stories and other written texts, has attempted to identify the different types of structure that hold our knowledge about the world in long-term memory. The best known of these structures are *scripts*, which describe stereotyped sequences of events, such as plane flights, visits to restaurants, or visits to doctors or dentists. We do, of course, have information about such sequences stored in our minds, but to spell out this information is no more to be a cognitive scientist than to produce a list of chemicals is to be a chemist. A scientific account of the organisation of memory should not just say what its organisation is, it should provide a framework within which we can explain how that organisation arises and what it makes possible.

SOME PSYCHOLOGICAL IDEAS ABOUT MEMORY

Since memory (along with attention) was at the forefront of human experimental psychology in the 1950s, it was one of the first topics to which the idea of information processing was applied. This idea has several facets, of which the most important for cognitive science is the notion stressed in chapter 1 – that mental processes are computations. However, memory research was influenced not so much by this idea, as by the idea that mental processes can be represented using flow charts of the kind used by engineers, and by computer scientists in the early stages of program development. A flow diagram model of a cognitive system divides that system into simpler subcomponents and shows how information is transmitted around the system.

Flow charts of cognitive functions can be complex, but the early models of memory and of attention were simple. The most influential early model of human memory – so influential that it is called the modal model – divides memory into two main components, a short-term store (STS) and a long-term store (LTS). STS is used, for example, to remember telephone numbers while we look away from the directory to dial them, while LTS holds information in a more permanent form. If a telephone number is more than about seven digits long, we have difficulty remembering it and have to look back at the directory. And if we need to remember the number while we walk to the telephone, we have to repeat it either aloud or to ourselves – we have to rehearse it. According to the modal model, all information first enters STS, from which it may pass to LTS. If we do not think we will need a particular telephone number again, it may never enter LTS. The modal model does not, of course, rest only on the observation that we have difficulty remembering telephone numbers. It is also supported by a wide range of experimental and clinical evidence.

One of the principal pieces of experimental evidence for the modal model was the *serial position effect in free recall*. If a person is shown a list of, say, 20 words and then asked to write down as many as they can remember ('free recall'), they are more likely to get the last few words right than the ones before them. The effect disappears if they have to do something else (count backwards in threes from 564 for a few seconds, for example) at the end of the list, before recall. The modal model explains this finding by claiming that the last few words in the list, and only those, are in STS when you get to the end of the list, and while you count backwards they are lost. Recent evidence has, however, cast doubt on this interpretation of the serial position effect, since the effect is restored if you also have to count backwards in threes between each word in the list – it depends on equal spacing.

The clinical evidence for the STS–LTS distinction is, perhaps, more intriguing than the experimental evidence. When people suffer from severe concussion, perhaps following an accident, they cannot remember the events before the accident. Over a period of time they regain their memories, with earlier memories (long before the concussion) coming back first. However, there is always a short period of time, just before the concussion, that they never remember. The explanation is not, of course, that they did not register what happened. Rather, it has been suggested, what happened then did not have the chance to be properly encoded into LTS and was never permanently recorded. How a blow to the head prevents this permanent recording is not properly understood, though a similar loss of memory is reported by psychiatric patients who are give electro-convulsive therapy (ECT), in which a (strictly controlled!) electric current is passed through the brain, usually in an attempt to relieve severe depression.

Another kind of clinical evidence for the distinction between STS and LTS comes from studies of patients with brain damage. Some patients appear to have lost their LTS, or at least the ability to add new information to it, while still having a normal STS. More rarely, there are patients whose long-term memory is good, but who can only remember about two digits at a time. The fact that each of the stores can be independently affected – a phenomenon known as *double dissociation* – suggests that they are anatomically, and therefore presumably functionally, separate.

The musician Clive Waring is an example of a person with very little ability to add facts to his long-term store, but whose short-term store is apparently normal. As we have already seen, Waring cannot remember things that happened a few minutes ago. But he can take part in conversations – he can remember what has been said to him long enough to formulate a reply. This ability clearly requires short-term storage of information, probably by a system rather more complex than one that is used to remember seven-digit phone numbers.

The most famous patient with an impaired LTS but an intact STS is known in the psychological literature by the initials HM, and was studied over a long period by Brenda Milner. HM suffered from severe epilepsy and had parts of his brain surgically removed in an attempt to control his fits. The parts removed included the hippocampus – a structure buried deep in the brain that gets its name from the fact that it looks like a seahorse (*hippocampus* is Latin for seahorse). HM's operation brought his epilepsy under control but had the unforeseen consequence that he was unable to remember events that happened to him, or that he heard about in newspapers or on TV, after the operation. For example, in 30 years HM never remembered Brenda Milner from one test session to the next. However, standard tests show that HM, like Clive Waring, has a normal short-term memory. Just like you or me, he can repeat back about seven digits accurately.

Patients with a defective STS but intact LTS do not provide such clear support for the modal model. Indeed, they pose a number of problems for it. The first is that, if information enters LTS via STS, these patients should have difficulty storing information in LTS. More generally, if STS is the system that supports conscious activity, which many people assume it is, these patients should be unconscious. Part of the solution to this problem is suggested by a closer examination of these patients' problems. They do not have a *global* short-term memory deficit. The best known of them, KF, who has been studied by Tim Shallice and Elizabeth Warrington, has a grossly impaired *auditory* short-term memory. He can only repeat back one or two digits. However, his memory for visually presented digits is much better – four or five items. Therefore, KF has a reasonable, if not completely normal, STS, which may be sufficient to allow information to enter LTS. However, this solution gives rise to a second problem. In the modal model, STS is a single store. KF's symptoms suggest it has at least two components, auditory and visual, that can be selectively damaged. Indeed, the idea that there is a unitary short-term memory store is no longer widely held.

Proponents of the modal model have always recognised the existence of (at least) two additional *very short-term* memory stores. These stores, used for seeing and hearing respectively, are known as *iconic* and *echoic* memory. The term 'echoic' suggests how the auditory store works – we remember what we have just heard as though it were echoing in our ears. The operation of these *sensory* memories is illustrated in a famous experiment by George Sperling. Sperling showed his subjects three rows of four letters for a twentieth of a second, followed by a pattern to prevent the persistence of the visual image. With such a brief display, people remember about four of the letters. However, if the display is followed by a sound of high, medium or low pitch – to indicate the top, middle or bottom row of letters – all four letters in the line are remembered. A certain amount of information (about four letters) can be extracted from the iconic store before it fades, and we have control over which part is extracted. However, since the subjects did not know which line would be signalled, information about all twelve letters must have been available, at least for a short period. By increasing the time between the end of the visual display and the tone, Sperling estimated that information in the iconic store lasted for about a quarter of a second. At that point as much information as can be has been transferred to STS, and the rest has been lost.

No one has claimed that KF has an intact iconic memory but a damaged echoic memory. The argument is, rather, that within *STS* a distinction must be made between visual and auditory storage. Indeed, there are a number of reasons for thinking that our short-term memory stores are more complex than the modal model, with its simple STS, suggests. I will present two arguments. First, there is considerable disagreement about how much information can be kept in short-term memory and how long it can be kept there. We can only remember telephone numbers of about seven digits and, unless we repeat them to ourselves, we can only remember them for a few seconds. However, detailed models of how, for example, we understand sentences or solve problems require short-term stores that can hold more complex information than a seven-digit number. Second, the length of the amnesic period before a concussion is hard to reconcile with a short-term store that can only hold information for a few seconds.

The first of these arguments against the simple STS of the modal model led Alan Baddeley and Graham Hitch to formulate the concept of *working memory*. By using the epithet *working*, Baddeley and Hitch emphasised that short-term memory is not simply a place where information is stored, but a place where it is worked on – a place where information is *processed*. Baddeley and Hitch, therefore, divide working memory into a *central executive*, that oversees the work taking place in the memory system, and specialised information stores. The two specialised stores that have been described in detail are the *articulatory loop* (in which a small amount of verbal material can be kept active by subvocal rehearsal) and the *visuospatial scratch pad* (which maintains visuo-spatial information). The separation of these two stores in the working memory model corresponds to the distinction between visual and auditory components of short-term memory.

Despite the wealth of evidence supporting the distinction between long- and short-term stores, the modal model went out of favour in the early 1970s, partly because its focus on storage rather than processing was inappropriate, particularly for short-term memory. Baddeley and Hitch's working memory model was one alternative in which processing was given a more central place. A more radical alternative, which effectively ignored questions about storage, was Fergus Craik and Robert Lockhart's idea of *levels of processing*, though this idea was never incorporated into a detailed memory model. According to Craik and Lockhart the main explanatory principle in a theory of human memory is that the deeper the level to which something is processed, the better it is remembered. This idea sounds plausible, but it encountered two problems. First, it was difficult to find an independent measure of how deeply something had been processed, other than how well it was remembered, so the theory's central claim was found to be circular. Second, it was never clear how the difference between long- and short-term stores could be accommodated in this framework.

The idea that there are different types of memory, though no particular psychological account, is supported by the computer metaphor for the mind and by the way computers work. We have already noted that human long-term memory corresponds roughly to the disc system of a home computer, though it works differently. The two other kinds of memory that home computer owners are likely to be familiar with are ROM (Read Only Memory) and RAM (the letters stand for Random Access Memory, but Read and Write Memory is a better name). ROMs hold frequently used programs. In one sense they are unnecessary, since a program can always be read from a disc into RAM when it is needed. However, ROM is a better metaphor than disc + RAM for many human abilities – the human brain contains many special purpose 'modules', for example the parts of the visual system we discussed in the last chapter. Unlike the visual system, a home computer is a general purpose machine. One moment it is used as a word processor, the next for playing a game, the next for balancing a bank account. For such flexibility a large general purpose memory (RAM) is useful. Programs are read from discs into RAM when required. RAM is also used to store the data on which the program works – the text for a word processor or the debits and credits for a bank account, so RAM and disc can both be used for relatively long-term storage of information. Indeed, many home computer systems now encourage their users to think of part of RAM as a disc. However, those users have to be careful, since information is lost from RAM when the computer is turned off. RAM differs from disc in that it can be used for processing as well as storage – programs can run in RAM, but not on disc. Since the brain cannot be 'turned off', the distinction between RAM and disc is not crucial for cognitive science, though the distinction between passive storage and active processing is.

Computers also use very short-term, very low-capacity memory stores called *registers*, though you are unlikely to hear about them, unless you program in assembly language or machine code. A register holds the intermediate results of a computation and its contents are overwritten, for example each time a new addition sum is done. In this sense registers are like the temporary memories that people use, though they hold less information, and the information does not decay if it is not overwritten. Programs can also use any part of the general purpose RAM as a temporary memory, so the short-term stores that computers use are different from those that people have. Thus, although the computer analogy is helpful in thinking about memory, there are many facts about human memory that it does not explain.

ECOLOGICAL VALIDITY

For many reasons the research described so far might look strange to the layperson. One is that memory was one of the first phenomena to be studied in experimental psychology, and it is therefore one in which the scientific concerns of psychologists are furthest removed from those of everyday life. Beginning with the work of Ebbinghaus at the end of the last century, and continuing through to the 1960s, memory was the central concern of human experimental psychology. Ebbinghaus tried to study memory in its pure form, unaffected by meaning, by teaching himself lists of three-letter nonsense syllables, such as CAZ. The idea that memory could be studied independently of what had to be remembered persisted through to the so-called 'verbal learning' research of the 1950s and 1960s. This research was inspired by two behaviourist ideas: first, that all learning is the learning of simple associations (*this* goes, or usually goes, with *that*), and second that a person's memory is a huge collection of associations between things they know about. In verbal learning research, memory was studied using the paired-associate paradigm, in which subjects have to learn arbitrary associations between familiar words (e.g. in this particular list *table* goes with *brother*).

The 'cognitive revolution' in psychology made people realise that this research was not very interesting. But there are two aspects of its dullness that are not always clearly distinguished. First, there is little intrinsic interest in how people learn lists of nonsense syllables, or lists of unrelated words, or lists of arbitrary pairs of words. However, as we saw in chapter 1, science does not necessarily concern itself with facts that are interesting in themselves. It needs facts that bear, however indirectly, on theoretically important issues. The second problem with verbal learning research was that, in the end, its findings could not be related to important issues – they did not tell us much about the interesting aspects of human memory.

One response to these problems is to demand that studies of memory be *ecologically valid*. Part of the reason, it has been claimed, why verbal learning studies were largely irrelevant to the normal workings of human memory is that they did not investigate its everyday uses. They took no account of the environment in which it has evolved. Ecologically valid experiments study memory 'in its natural habitat'. Their subject matter might be 'autobiographical memory' or 'everyday memory'. Although much of this research is descriptive, it has produced many interesting findings, some of which are discussed below. However, cognitive scientists need not restrict themselves to ecologically valid studies.

One might claim that any cognitive skill should be investigated in an ecologically valid way. Part of the reason why the argument has been particularly popular in memory research is, I believe, that throughout the 1960s and 1970s memory research lost its central place in human experimental psychology and its practitioners began to feel defensive. Scientists are most prone to methodological discussions when they are not making satisfactory progress.

The argument for ecologically valid experiments is plausible, but we can see that it is invalid by looking at the way other sciences work. Although findings in sciences such as physics and physiology often seem boring to a non-specialist, their practitioners do not feel tempted to study particles of matter or living organisms 'in their natural environment'. Rather, they try *to bridge the gap between the laboratory and the real world* by constructing theories that on the one hand apply to ordinary phenomena and on the other hand make predictions about what should happen in controlled laboratory experiments. Thus physicists and physiologists make the distinction, if only implicitly, between the two reasons why research findings can seem dull. And while I would not wish to claim that cognitive science must be like other sciences, cognitive scientists would be foolish if they thought they could not learn from them.

Physicists subject natural materials to conditions that are rarely encountered in the real world. Physiologists do the same to living matter. By doing so they hope to learn something of general scientific interest. Perhaps to construct a theory that, among other things, explains the everyday behaviour of inanimate or animate matter in an elegant way. Investigating, say, the properties of solids at very low temperatures does not tells us anything *directly* about their behaviour under the circumstances in which we normally encounter them (ambient temperature and pressure). But if experiments are important, they will contribute to a general understanding of physical or physiological phenomena. Similarly, experiments on human memory need not investigate memory in everyday circumstances, though some of them might. However, to give interest and importance to experimental results, there must be some connection, perhaps direct, perhaps very indirect, between the experiment and how we ordinarily remember things.

HOW OUR MEMORIES FAIL US

At home I get into trouble for forgetting to do things, both in the short term – I forget to bring downstairs something I have been asked to bring down – and in the intermediate term – I forget that last night I was asked to bring home something from the office today. Most people are prone to such lapses of memory; some do more about it than others. Another of my failings is forgetting the name of someone I have just been introduced to, even though my memory for names in the longer term has been described as remarkably good. Such lapses can be highly embarrassing and can be avoided using a technique advocated in 'How to Succeed' books. The trick is to make sure you learn the name, either by repeating it back to yourself or by making a connection between the name and some characteristic of the person. One usually fails to learn names because one has no strong motive for learning them. 'How to Succeed' books combine a simple social psychological principle (taking an interest in someone, for example by learning their name, usually produces a positive response) with a simple principle from cognitive science (if you're motivated to learn something you usually will).

To remember things in the intermediate and longer term we use *external memory aids* such as scoreboards, diaries, calendars, shopping lists, and manuals. Indeed, one of the failings of cognitive science, with its emphasis on what goes on in the mind, is its lack of an account of the essential role that such external aids play in cognitive processing.

So far we have been talking about one particular way in which our memories are bad. We forget to do things when we were supposed to. But when we are chastised for not doing them, we usually remember being asked. We have stored the right information in memory, but we have not retrieved it at the right time. Another way in which our memories are bad is that they distort what happened, and in ways that are difficult to detect. The reason why the distortions are difficult to detect is that memories are often vivid and they come readily to mind. These properties of memories suggest, at least to the person who has them, that they are correct. Sometimes memories can be checked against objective records, but most of the time we do not bother.

A famous case of distortions in memory – one studied by the cognitive psychologist Ulric Neisser – is that of John Dean's testimony at the Watergate hearings. Before the notorious Watergate tapes became available, Dean reported conversations he had had with President Richard Nixon in great detail. When Dean's testimony was compared with the tapes it was found to be highly inaccurate in detail and often untrue to the structure of the real conversation. However, the conversations he 'reconstructed' almost always gave an accurate picture of the underlying state of affairs.

A particularly interesting case of distortion is that of unreliable *flashbulb memories*. Flashbulb memories are memories of what we were doing when some momentous or surprising event happened. For Americans, on whom most flashbulb memory research has been carried out, the prototypical event of this kind is the assassination of President Kennedy. Flashbulb memories are so-called because they are particularly vivid. It is as if we remember a scene frozen in the 'flash' created by the momentous event. The vividness of these memories strongly inclines people who have them to regard them as accurate. For the most part they are, but vividness provides no guarantee of accuracy. Ulric Neisser has described how he was able to show that one of his own flashbulb memories was inaccurate. The memory in question was of what Neisser was doing when he heard the news of the bombing of Pearl Harbour, which brought the United States into the Second World War. He had for years believed that he was listening to a baseball game on the radio. Eventually he realised that, since Pearl Harbour was bombed in December and baseball is a summer game, the memory must have been mistaken. Neisser was actually listening to an American football game, but it so happened that the venue and the names of the teams were likely to suggest baseball.

Distortions in memory are also found in eyewitness testimony in criminal proceedings. The research of Elizabeth Loftus and others on this topic suggests a number of conclusions that should have a profound impact on the way such testimony is treated in court. First, our preconceptions about eyewitness testimony – its folk psychology – are inaccurate in many details. For example, people think that violent crimes should be remembered more accurately than non-violent ones. Experimental work with videotaped mock crimes suggests the opposite is true. Other aspects of our folk psychology are correct. People are highly susceptible to leading questions and they are much poorer at recognising people from racial groups other than their own. However, this effect is not, as one might be tempted to suppose, increased by racial prejudice.

There are various reasons why memories are distorted. According to Neisser, his flashbulb memory was distorted because of the importance of baseball (as opposed to football) to him, and because he wanted to establish his identity as an American – baseball is more quintessentially American than American football. John Dean both overestimated his own ability to remember details of conversations and changed his own role in the events that led up to Watergate into what he thought it should have been. Eyewitnesses often fail to encode the relevant information about a crime and use whatever clues they can to reconstruct what happened. If those clues are misleading, eyewitnesses will be misled. The fact they are so easily misled shows how much of our memory is reconstructive.

The reconstructive aspects of memory are clearly illustrated in an old study by Sir Frederic Bartlett, and reported in his 1932 book *Remembering*. Bartlett was the major figure in a tradition that opposed Ebbinghaus – one that emphasised the importance of content in memory. In a series of studies Bartlett investigated how students at Cambridge remembered an American Indian story called 'War of the Ghosts'. The story is as follows:

One night two young men from Egulac went down to the river to hunt seals, and while they were there it became foggy and calm. Then they heard war-cries, and they thought: 'Maybe this is a war-party'. They escaped to the shore, and hid behind a log. Now canoes came up, and they heard the noise of paddles, and saw one canoe coming up to them. There were five men in the canoe, and they said:

'What do you think? We wish to take you along. We are going up the river to make war on the people'.

One of the young men said: 'I have no arrows'.

'Arrows are in the canoe', they said.

'I will not go along. I might be killed. My relatives do not know where I have gone. But you', he said, turning to the other, 'may go with them'.

So one of the young men went, but the other returned home.

And the warriors went on up the river to a town on the other side of Kalama. The people came down to the water and they began to fight, and many were killed. But presently the young man heard one of the warriors say: 'Quick, let us go home: that Indian has been hit'. Now he thought: 'Oh, they are ghosts'. He did not feel sick, but they said he had been shot.

So the canoes went back to Egulac, and the young man went ashore to his house, and made a fire. And he told everybody and said: 'Behold I accompanied the ghosts, and we went to fight. Many of our fellows were killed, and many of those who attacked us were killed. They said I was hit, and I did not feel sick'.

He told it all, and then he became quiet. When the sun rose he fell down. Something black came out of his mouth. His face became contorted. The people jumped up and cried.

He was dead.

Both in style and in incident 'War of the Ghosts' is somewhat alien to English readers. A number of details of the story do not make immediate sense. In the students' reproductions these details were often changed into a more comprehensible form, or omitted altogether. One of the most problematic aspects of the story was the following: the young man's being hit was the reason for ceasing hostilities, yet he was not dead at that point, though others of the party were. Despite the young man's explicit 'Oh, they are ghosts' and his later 'I accompanied the ghosts', many subjects removed this supernatural element from the story. One took The Ghosts (with capital letters) to be the name of a clan, for example, and another had the young man thinking he was seeing ghosts when he was hit. In more prosaic ways, too, the story was simplified. The 'canoes' became 'boats' in many of the reproductions, and 'paddling' became 'rowing'.

To explain these distortions, which became more marked as time passed, Bartlett proposed that remembering is not simply a matter of reading out information from memory, as it usually is in a computer. Rather, it is a *reconstructive process* in which both the recollection of a particular incident and general knowledge are combined. In Bartlett's study the relevant incidents are those in 'War of the Ghosts', and because that story was difficult for parochial 1920s Englishmen to understand, they did not remember its details well. Indeed, they may never have encoded those details that did not make sense. The reconstructive mental processes of a student trying to remember part of the story might have been as follows: I remember something about boats on a river, so they must have been rowed, because that is how boats are usually propelled along a river. These processes are unconscious and the students would probably not have been aware that their memory of the story was inaccurate. In such reconstructions, general knowledge supplements the fragmentary memory for the story to produce a coherent but inaccurate version of it. In stories from one's own culture, however, to which one's general knowledge is more appropriate, reconstruction produces, or rather *reproduces*, something close to the original story.

IMPLICIT AND EXPLICIT MEMORY AND KNOWLEDGE

When we talk about memory in the everyday sense we mean bringing past events, or at least what we take to be past events, back into consciousness. However, one of the major lessons of cognitive science is that much of our behaviour is governed by information that is stored in our minds, but of which we cannot normally become conscious. Only by becoming cognitive scientists and formulating explicit theories about that knowledge do we find out what we know! This idea runs throughout this book. For example, in the last chapter we saw that our visual systems embody general principles for interpreting the images on our retinas – principles that reflect knowledge of what the world is like. Similarly, our ability to use language depends on stored information about the language we speak. Furthermore, cognitive scientists typically refer to this information or these principles as *knowledge* and speak of it as being stored in our memory. Another term for this knowledge that we cannot ordinarily bring into consciousness is *implicit knowledge*.

A related distinction, between explicit and implicit memory, has recently become important in memory research. An explicit memory of something is a memory in the everyday sense. Something is implicitly remembered if we have no recollection of it but if our past experience of it affects our current behaviour. For example, amnesic patients may protest that they have never seen a particular puzzle before. Like HM they may even not remember the experimenter from one session to the next. Nevertheless, the second time they are given the puzzle, they solve it more quickly than the first time. They do not consciously remember the puzzle, but solving it the first time helps them to solve it the second time. Implicit memory is also readily demonstrated in normal people.

Consciousness is one of the most perplexing problems for cognitive science, and it is not one that cognitive scientists have made much progress on. They cannot even agree on whether it is a legitimate topic of study. Before this recent work on explicit and implicit memory, the distinction between explicit knowledge that can be brought into consciousness and implicit knowledge was not, therefore, of great importance in cognitive science. Indeed, workers in AI, who are largely responsible for ideas about how knowledge is stored in the mind, have ignored the distinction. Their programs have not exhibited consciousness and they have found no reason to believe that explicit and implicit information are stored in the brain in different ways. Whether knowledge is implicit or explicit probably depends only on what other mental processes have access to it.

FURTHER READING

Alan Parkin's *Memory and Amnesia* (Basil Blackwell, 1987) and Alan Baddeley's *Your Memory: A User's Guide* (Penguin, 1983) are both approachable introductions to the psychological study of memory and its disorders.

4   Language

Language is another cognitive faculty that most of us take for granted. Not only do we speak and understand what is said to us without conscious effort, but as children we acquire the ability to speak with ease. What child ever complained of being tired from learning too many new words! Reading and writing are different. In many parts of the world, these skills are still comparatively rare. Even in our own culture some people never acquire the facility with written language that they enjoy with spoken language. And everyone has to be *taught* to read and write. Nevertheless, if you are reading this book, you probably take literacy for granted. You do not ask the questions cognitive scientists ask. What makes these skills possible? What information do we use to understand a sentence? How much of that information is in the 'input' and how much is stored information that we use to process that input? How should we characterise the state of having understood a sentence? What information can a child bring to bear on the problem of learning a language?

There are situations that make us realise how complicated language understanding is. I am in one of them now. I am writing this chapter in Tilburg in the Netherlands, and I do not know Dutch very well. When I first came here I could make virtually nothing of spoken Dutch. It sounded like a continuous babble. I certainly did not know where one word stopped and the next started. Unfamiliar languages sound like that and, when you think about it, it is surprising, because we feel that utterances in our own language are clearly divided into words. Modern instruments that allow speech, or any other sound, to be analysed confirm what this observation suggests – very often there is no break between spoken words and the sound *is* continuous. There are pauses in speech, and they almost always occur between words, not in the middle of them. But many words have no gap between them. So one question for a theory of language processing to answer is: how do we divide a continuous sound pattern into separate words?

LANGUAGE USE BY ADULTS

We know that languages have rules. To start with there are those irritating rules of English spelling that have so many exceptions. And those of us who have learned, or tried to learn, a foreign language know that languages differ from one another in seemingly arbitrary ways, and that you have to learn the rules, whether they be the declensions and conjugations of Latin and Greek or the noun-adjective concord rules of French. As aspiring francophones we envy the ease with which native French speakers almost always get the gender of the nouns right and then 'remember' to make the adjectives agree. This fact suggests the following pertinent observation: the rule system we are struggling to learn is, in some sense, part of the mental equipment of native French speakers. Yet French men and women may be hardly aware of that rule system and they certainly do not *consciously* use it when they are speaking. Like any other well practised skill, language use is highly automated.

Linguists have shown, particularly in the last thirty years, how complicated the system of rules needed to describe a language is. There are many types of rules. Rules about the sounds of the language, for example – about which physically different noises count as the same sound. A man, a woman and a child say *red* in different ways, and all three sound different when they are standing next to us, when they are in the next room, and when they are talking on the telephone. Yet the noise they make is identified as the same word. Physical measurements would show that the *red* of a man standing next to us is more like his *led* than it is like the *red* of a woman on the telephone. Yet we call the man's utterances different words. A Japanese speaker, on the other hand, will have difficulty distinguishing any *red* from any *led*, since Japanese does not have pairs of words like *red* and *led* that differ only in that one has an R sound where the other has an L sound.

Languages also have rules about how sounds can be put together to make words. How do you know that *btir* not only isn't an English word, but that it cannot be one? Because English words cannot begin with a B sound followed by a T sound. This rule might seem a natural one, because words like *btir* would be difficult to say. But words in foreign languages are often difficult to pronounce – think of the consonant clusters at the end of Polish words for example. In fact, many languages have words that start with bt-. Other rules, again specific to particular languages, tell us how to make complex words out of simpler ones (add -er to a verb to get the name of someone who performs the activity named by the verb: *build – builder, climb – climber, paint – painter*), how to combine words to form phrases, clause and sentences, and how to work out what a sentence means from the meanings of its parts.

We are not aware of these rules when we use language. Indeed, we often cannot formulate them, and patient linguistic research is needed to uncover them. But, as I pointed out earlier, these rules govern our use of language. We usually behave as if we were following them, and when we do not, we admit that we haven't said things as well as we might have. So, German speakers automatically put past participles at the end of sentences, whereas English speakers put them after the auxiliary verb (*I have eaten the apple* vs. *Ich habe den Apfel gegessen*), and Germans put the verb at the end in subordinate clauses (*Because I have eaten the apple* vs. *Weil ich den Apfel gegessen habe*). As we saw in chapter 1, many linguists believe that in setting out the rules for a language, its *grammar* in the technical sense of that term, they have also described part of the mental apparatus of speakers of that language, which they use, usually unconsciously, in speaking, listening, reading, and writing.

Whatever their views, everyone agrees that language use is a cognitive ability that depends on a store of specialised information in long-term memory – information specifically about language. Furthermore, they agree that there are parallels between the information in this store and linguistic grammars, though not everyone thinks that the parallels are as direct as the influential linguist Noam Chomsky. Everyone also agrees that non-specialised knowledge is important in understanding language. In particular, knowledge about the subject matter under discussion plays a role in language use, since speakers and writers often rely on listeners and readers to provide details that are implicit in the text. However, there is some disagreement about where specialised knowledge about language ends and where more general cognitive abilities begin.

Comprehension and production

Language is a means of conveying information from one person to another. There are, therefore, two complementary aspects of our ability to use language: the ability to express our ideas in speech or writing (language production) and the ability to understand the ideas expressed by others (language comprehension). These abilities are highly automated in normal adults. We have little conscious awareness of the cognitive processes that contribute to them. So, as in other similar cases, folk psychology has little to say about them.

To construct a theory of how people use language we need to describe a 'mechanism' (in the usual very general sense) that embodies the rules of a language, that can produce and/or understand sentences and that can fit them into, or work out their role in, longer discourses and texts. We also need to describe how this mechanism relates to our other mental faculties. We do not say things at random; we say things that derive from our goals and desires, and from what is happening around us. We need to explain how our ability to use language subserves our more general concerns.

Cognitive scientists usually assume that the messages people want to convey can be characterised more or less independently of the language in which they are to be expressed, although there is some disagreement about the extent to which our conceptual systems are untainted by the language we use. The problem in language production is, therefore, to select the contextually appropriate linguistic form to express the message one wants to convey, and then to express that form in speech or writing. The problem in language comprehension is to identify the linguistic form, and then to extract the intended message from it together with information about the context in which it was used.

Comprehension has been more intensively studied in cognitive science than production so we will consider it first, outlining the main processes that contribute to our ability to understand language. We cannot help hearing a clearly spoken English word or seeing a printed version of it as that word. However, a small step back from our everyday concerns shows that, despite the ease with which we normally identify words, recognition is a complex process. When we hear a language we do not know, we may recognise some sounds (a B sound here, an R sound there). When we see a printed word from that language we may recognise its letters if they are from the Roman alphabet, or we may just see lines and curves if the word is a Chinese ideogram or in Arabic script. But such words have not been identified. Spoken words are initially vibrations in the air impinging on the ear drum, and written words are typically patterns of black marks on white paper creating a pattern of activity in the retinal cells. In language understanding, words are first subject to the kind of perceptual processing discussed in chapter 2.

Why is looking at an English word different from looking at an ideogram? The visual patterns are the same for us as they are for a Chinese speaker. What makes the difference is our knowledge about English words and how they are written. Cognitive scientists call this store of knowledge the *mental lexicon*, and we are very good at getting information out of it. Although our reading vocabulary contains tens of thousands of words, we can extract information about several hundred of them a minute – in ordinary reading of light material we read five or more words a second. To recognise a printed word we have to find out which of the words we know can have the appearance of the pattern in front of us. It could be any one of them, so we must be able to use the information in the mental lexicon very efficiently. There are two main ideas about how we do so. One is that we search through the entries until we find a match for the current visual or auditory pattern.

The other is that there is a separate detector for each word that is always on the look-out for that word. Although searching through every entry may seem impossible, given the speed at which words are recognised, it is not. We have already seen that complex computations can take place rapidly. Furthermore, spelling checkers on even fairly modest home computers can check in a minute or two each of several thousand words in a lengthy document to see if they are in its dictionary.

Spelling checkers show that, given a clear description of a word, in this case in terms of its letters, deciding whether it is in a lexicon is straightforward. In understanding language one doesn't simply want to know if a word is in the mental lexicon, but needs to make its meaning available. However, it is a trivial matter, though it requires a lot of extra memory, to add the meaning of each word to its lexical entry.

A major problem for cognitive science is to work out what properties of the 'stimulus' people use to recognise words. This problem is most easily solved for printed words, a fact that partly explains why research on the recognition of spoken words addresses different questions from that on written words. One problem in recognising spoken words is that the speech sounds that correspond roughly to letters do not have a constant form. They are like handwritten letters, rather than printed ones, only more so. Vowel sounds depend on which consonants they come between and, conversely, consonants are affected by surrounding vowels. Not only that, spoken words change in ways that we are not aware of. If you say the word *molten* slowly and clearly there is one sound corresponding to each letter. However, in rapid, casual speech the word may come out more like *mot' n*. Add to this the fact mentioned at the beginning of the chapter, that speech often contains no explicit clue to where one word begins and another ends, and it is clear that the problem of identifying sounds at the ear with words in the mental lexicon is a very difficult one.

Cognitive science also has to account for a wide range of facts about how people recognise words – facts that have been discovered largely in the psychological investigation of written word identification. For example, common words are processed more quickly than rare ones. So, in search models of word recognition the entries in the mental lexicon are checked in order of the frequency with which the words are used. Another example: words are recognised more quickly when they are presented with or just after a related word (table – chair, cat – dog, black – white), but this effect is larger for rare words than for common ones. Any viable model of word identification must be able to explain these facts.

I have already noted that checking that a word is in one's mental lexicon is not (usually) an end in itself. The point is to make its meaning available for understanding what is being said or read. It is worth emphasising that

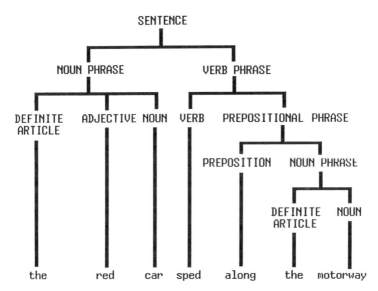

Figure 4.1 The structure of the sentence *The red car sped along the motorway*

every word has to be looked up. We think of a dictionary (or lexicon) as something we only use when we come across a word we don't know. The mental lexicon differs in this respect from an ordinary dictionary. When we see the visual pattern *dog* we have to identify it as the word *dog* and, thence, we bring to mind a certain kind of animal.

Bringing word meanings to mind is not enough for understanding a sentence. Those meanings have to be combined to produce larger chunks of meaning. How? Part of the answer is that words are grouped into phrases according to what parts of speech they belong to. Like an ordinary dictionary, the mental lexicon contains information about the parts of speech of the words in it, and that information is available once a word has been identified. Consider a very simple example: the three words *the red car* in that order. *The* is a definite article, *red* is an adjective, and *car* is a noun. It is a rule about the structure of English sentences that a definite article followed by an adjective followed by a noun makes up one kind of noun phrase, so *the red car* is a noun phrase. Of course, not all sequences of three consecutive words in a sentence make up a phrase. In *The red car sped along the motorway, car sped along* is not a phrase. Even simple sentences have a complicated arrangement of phrases within phrases, as figure 4.1, which is typical of those used by linguists, illustrates. For example, *the motorway*, which is itself a noun phrase, is part of the prepositional phrase *along the motorway*, and that phrase in turn is part of the verb phrase *sped along the motorway*.

Grouping words into phrases, and phrases within phrases, is called *parsing*. It is not the same as working out the meaning of a sentence. But it is an important step to working out the meaning. It is another example of the way a cognitive process can use stored information to analyse incoming data. The incoming data is a (possibly completely novel) sequence of words. The stored knowledge is knowledge about what parts of speech those words are and what kinds of phrases and sentences the language allows.

I have used a straightforward case as an illustration. In general, a sequence of words will be difficult to parse, because a word may belong to several parts of speech (think of all the nouns in English that can also be verbs), or because the same words can be grouped in different ways and we don't know which to choose. For example, in *after he left the lab* the main break could be after *lab*, as it would be if the sentence continued *there was a fire*, or after *left*, in which case the sentence might continue ...*caught fire*.

The mathematical analysis of parsing, developed by computer scientists who have to ensure that what is typed at a computer terminal is interpreted precisely, is highly complex. And there is considerable debate about how it should be applied to human parsing of natural languages.

The most fundamental question is to what extent understanding speech and writing requires parsing. It is easy to think of methods that might be used to avoid detailed analysis of the structure of a sentence. For example, consider the (relatively) complex sentence *The cat the dog chased miaowed*. The sentence mentions a cat and a dog and two things that happened, chasing and miaowing. One way to understand this sentence would be to think of the most plausible connection between the animals and the things that happened. Cats miaow, not dogs, and dogs more often chase cats, so folklore tells us, than cats chase dogs. So the sentence is about a dog chasing a cat and the cat miaowing. Correct! But what about the sentence *The dog the cat chased miaowed*. That sentence describes an unlikely event, yet there is nothing wrong with it as a sentence. Nor is there any doubt about what it should mean. Yet, if we reasoned as above, we would conclude – but this time wrongly – that the dog chased the cat and the cat miaowed. When a sentence describes unlikely events, or even ones that are impossible in the real world, like dogs miaowing, we have to use its structure to work out its meaning. If we are to avoid misunderstanding descriptions of unlikely events, we cannot avoid parsing at least some sentences.

We have to parse some sentences, so how do we use the rules about how phrases in our language can be constructed? Assuming that sentences are analysed more or less from 'left to right', two more specific questions can be asked. First, are analysis trees built from the words upwards (so-called 'bottom-up' analysis) or projected onto the words using predictions about the kinds of phrases that ought to be appearing ('top-down')? Second, are all possible analyses considered together ('breadth-first') or is a single one developed, that might eventually prove to be wrong ('depth-first')? Current thinking favours the view that the human sentence parsing mechanism works depth-first and, largely, in a bottom-up manner, but the issues are far from resolved.

What evidence suggests that parsing is depth-first? Consider a sentence that begins *I told the girl that I liked...* It might continue *... meeting her in the evening.* Or *... to meet me that evening.* In the first case *that I liked* is part of a so-called complement clause that specifies what I told the girl (I liked meeting her in the evening). In the second case it is a so-called relative clause that tells us which girl the sentence is about (the one that I liked). If we work depth-first on one analysis, say the complement clause one, up to the word *liked*, and if the sentence continues in a way that is not consistent with that analysis (*... to meet me that evening*), it should be difficult to understand the continuation. A number of experiments have supported this idea, thus favouring the depth-first theory. Why should the complement clause analysis be favoured? Because it is, in a technical sense, simpler.

Parsing is a step towards understanding a sentence, because the meaning of a sentence depends on the way its words are grouped into phrases, and on the relations between those phrases. We illustrated this fact above. In 'the dog the cat chased', *chased* is an ordinary active verb form, so its subject *the cat* is doing the chasing. And *the dog*, which is the so-called head noun of the relative clause, is getting chased.

Working out who did what is an important part of understanding a sentence. However, most of the more interesting and more difficult questions about how we understand conversations and monologues, books, newspapers and magazines are about how we put information from different sentences or utterances together. In chapter 1 I discussed pronouns, which tie information from different parts of the text together by signalling that something is being referred to again. Other ties are signalled by conjunctions such as *but*, *however*, *since*, *so*, and *because*. Others still depend on the tenses of the verbs. So, *John was walking round the corner. A car hooted* describes two concurrent events, while *John walked round the corner. A car hooted* describes two consecutive events. Some of these local ties and almost all global ones depend on knowledge about the world. To account for the use of such ties we need to know how knowledge about the world is organised and how it is accessed (see chapter 2). Indeed, since this knowledge is also used in everyday reasoning (see chapter 5), accounting for its organisation and use is one of the principal challenges for cognitive science. And, despite our great facility in using such knowledge, the challenge is proving very difficult.

What is the result of putting together information from different parts of a text? A broad answer is that readers and listeners have to construct a mental representation of the content of conversations they take part in or texts that they read. Since language is used to convey (or ask for) information about the world, the mental representation of the content of a text is not primarily a representation of its linguistic properties, but a representation of the part of the world that it is 'about' – regardless of whether it is a description, a question or a command. Such representations, which are called *mental models*, are similar to those constructed by perceptual processes and to those used in thinking and reasoning.

Language production – speaking and writing – parallels comprehension in many ways. Or perhaps 'mirrors' would be a better word, since a 'late' process in understanding, working out meaning, corresponds to an 'early' process in production, selecting a meaning to convey. The most obvious difference between production and comprehension is the need to *plan* one's productions. Speakers and writers have to plan at many levels. In many cases – writing a speech, a newspaper article or a book – the overall structure of the piece has to be considered. At a more detailed level the structure of each sentence and the way it links to what has gone before must be thought about. Even in casual conversations, which have no overall structure, we plan what we are going to say ahead of time, though we may not realise we are doing so. Indeed, studying hesitations and pauses can help to elucidate the process of planning.

Like comprehension, production makes use of the store of information about language that we have in long-term memory. Much of what we know about how this information is used in conversation has come from studying speech errors. Many people associate the psychological study of speech errors with Freud, who believed that they revealed thoughts suppressed by the conscious mind. Like most of Freud's views this one is difficult to substantiate. Psycholinguistic studies of speech errors show that most of them are perfectly innocent and reveal more about our linguistic knowledge than about our repressed thoughts. So, in a collection of speech errors that I assembled with some colleagues, someone who wanted to talk about *the new Mel Brooks film* started to say *the new Bel....* The B from the beginning of *Brooks* had moved forwards and taken the place of the M in Mel. This sort of error shows that in language production words are divided into individual sounds, which can take on a life of their own. Furthermore, sounds move only relatively small distances, suggesting that we convert our ideas into sounds in small chunks.

Other errors involve whole words. If you cannot decide which word to choose, you might blend two possibilities: *hilarity* and *hysterics* become *hilarics* in one of our examples. Or if you don't know how pointed to be, *girl* and *lesbian* might turn into *glesbian*. In other cases one word is substituted for another, to which it may be related in meaning (*pickers* for *growers*) or sound (*great* [hair] for *grey* [hair]). Assuming that these errors occur when the word selected from the mental lexicon is close to the one that was intended, they suggest that the lexicon is organised both by sound and by meaning.

LEARNING YOUR LANGUAGE

Another important question for cognitive science is: how do children learn language? Failure to learn spoken language is so rare that folk psychological explanations of language learning are limited to the few exceptions to this rule. Profound deafness makes spoken language hard to acquire, as does severe brain damage. Less severe handicaps have comparatively little effect, and are reflected in what handicapped people are able to discuss, rather than in their facility with language *per se*. Another fact that is part of most people's folk psychology is that, wherever a child is born, it will learn the language or languages of the people it grows up with. The Vietnamese orphans adopted by parents in the USA speak American English just like their classmates. They have no 'Vietnamese' accent. I, on the other hand, no matter how well I eventually learn Dutch, will always speak it with an English accent. Furthermore, I will have to work hard to learn it. I won't pick it up as a Dutch child will. Adults learn languages in a different way from children. Cognitive science must explain why and how. A related fact is that the tiny number of unfortunate children who are raised in an environment in which they experience no language are unable to learn more than the rudiments of one, and the older they are before their 'rescue' the more problems they have. Genie, a Californian girl born in 1957 who was locked in a closet between the ages of 2 and 13, had considerable difficulty learning about sentence structure and expressed her sometimes sophisticated meanings in rudimentary sentence forms.

Using mathematical techniques it is possible to ask how difficult a task language learning is. The answer, depending on the assumptions you make about what is learned, is either extremely difficult or impossible! This result suggests that much of what we know about language is not learned at all, but built into us, perhaps genetically. At first this idea seems implausible, since different languages are so different from one another. If information about one language, say English, is built in, it will be the wrong information for a West African child who has to learn Hausa or a Chinese child learning Mandarin. And since any child can learn any language equally well, it cannot be that different children have information about different languages built into them. Of course, no one claims they do. There are, for example, major differences between the vocabularies of different languages (*dog* vs. *chien* vs. *hund* vs. *hond* vs...), which have to be learned. In fact, children learn vocabulary very quickly. To acquire a vocabulary of 14,000 words by age six (a typical achievement) means learning on average nine new words a day over a period of four and a half years.

The point of built-in information is that it reduces the amount to be learned and therefore makes language learning as a whole easier. There are two main accounts of what is built in. Both assume that this information takes the form of a set of general principles that helps us to process appropriately the 'data' from which language has to be learned. Where the two versions differ is on the nature of the principles.

The first idea, put forward by the linguist Noam Chomsky, is that people have a special *language faculty* – a separate part of the mind responsible for dealing with language. He claims that this faculty has built into it information about what languages must be like. Despite the superficial differences (for example, in vocabulary) between languages, Chomsky argues that when linguists move to a more abstract level of description, languages have much in common – ways of putting together words to make phrases and sentences, for example. Twenty years ago it would have been easy to describe what Chomsky thought languages had in common, but over the years his ideas have become more refined and more abstract. It is hard to give a simple account that is true to the spirit of his recent ideas. However, the crucial point in Chomsky's theory is that what is built in is specific to language and is not part of a set of general cognitive abilities that might also be used in thinking and perceiving. Support for this idea comes from the fact that, for example, Genie's impairments were reasonably specific to language.

An alternative idea is that our ability to learn language *does* derive from more general cognitive abilities. And if it is just one facet of our general cognitive abilities, which we to some extent share with other 'higher' animals, it should be relatively straightforward to explain how that ability evolved. One way of trying to show that language is not specially human is to compare it with 'languages' that other animals use naturally or which they can be taught. For example, honey bees have a 'language' through which they can let other bees know where a source of food is in relation to the hive. This language takes the form of a 'dance' in which the direction of the food is signalled by the direction of movement on the surface of the hive and the distance of the food by the intensity of the dancing. However, unlike human languages this language is highly specific and inflexible (bees can't 'talk' about anything but food sources). Furthermore, whatever the truth about human language, the honey bees' dance is almost certainly innate.

There has always been speculation about whether animals might learn human languages – many stories are based on this idea. The apes are the most intelligent non-human animals and the ones most closely related to us. When serious attempts have been made to teach animals to talk, apes have been chosen. The early attempts were failures. The most sustained effort to teach a chimp, Vicki, to talk resulted in her being able to say just four words: *momma, poppa, up*, and *cup*. It was eventually realised that the problem lay not in chimps' linguistic abilities but in their ability to make speech-like sounds. Unlike budgerigars, parrots and mynah birds, chimps do not have the right vocal apparatus.

This observation, together with knowledge about the manual dexterity of chimps, led to the suggestion that chimps might be able to learn sign languages. So in 1966, Beatrice and Allen Gardner started to teach Ameslan (American Sign Language for the Deaf) to a young female chimp called Washoe. Washoe soon learned over 100 Ameslan signs, corresponding roughly to spoken words. She also produced sequences of signs that were like simple sentences, for example, *tickle me* and *come gimme sweet*.

Since 1966 a large number of chimps and other apes have learned both sign languages and languages based on plastic tokens or figures on a computer screen. This work has been highly controversial. On the one hand, some people argue that it has shown that language is not specifically human and that Chomsky's claim that there is an innate language faculty specific to people is wrong. Others go further and suggest that language is not innate at all. On the other hand critics argue that 'ape language' is irrelevant to human language, for two reasons. First, ape language lacks some of the crucial properties of human language, in particular the kind of hierarchical sentence structure discussed above. Second, even if apes did learn a language with all the features of human language, what has already been found out shows that they would learn it in a different and more laborious way than children. The necessity for this different type of learning, it is argued, supports the idea that apes cannot rely on an innate language-learning mechanism, whereas humans can.

Returning to human language learning, a further complication arises from an assumption made by many people who work in the field. This assumption is that children learn language from *positive examples only*. A positive example is a word, expression or sentence used correctly. To give a child a negative example would be to tell it explicitly it had said something that was (linguistically) incorrect or poor. The assumption is based on the fact that, although parents often tell their children when they say something untrue, they almost never correct the way that they express something. Furthermore, children are bad at learning from negative evidence. The following classic example was first reported by David McNeill. A child said *Nobody don't like me* and was told: *No, say 'nobody likes me.'* After several repetitions of this exchange, the child suddenly thought it had discovered its error and said: *Oh!*

Nobody, don't likes me. So it seems that children learn about things like verb endings and complex grammatical constructions simply by hearing (positive) examples of them.

Learning from positive examples is harder than learning from positive and negative examples, because it eliminates one potentially valuable source of information. Overgeneralisation, which is a common phenomenon in language acquisition, poses a particular problem for learning from positive examples only. One example of overgeneralisation occurs in the learning of the past tenses of English verbs. A child will first learn a few past tenses by rote: the common, irregular ones, such as *was, had, went*. Then it notices that some less common verbs follow a pattern (like – liked; suck – sucked; smack – smacked). On this basis it conjectures that there is a general rule, the – ed rule, which can be used to form past tenses. This rule generates forms such as *goed*. The child cannot reason that because there is a word *went*, which is the past tense of *go*, there can't be a word *goed*. Languages often have two words with roughly the same meaning – we call them synonyms. As those of you with children know, they do use forms such as *goed* at about three years – they overgeneralise the rule for past tenses. Why do children who say *goed* when they are three stop saying it, and revert to saying *went* by the time they are four or five? No positive example *by itself* can ever show that *goed* is wrong. Telling a child directly that *goed* is wrong would be to use it as a negative example. No convincing answer to this question has been proposed.

A final question that the rule-based nature of language raises for language acquisition is: can connectionist machines learn language? Connectionists argue that, although rules are not explicitly encoded into their machines, those machines can learn to behave as if they were following rules. Critics of connectionism argue that connectionist machines cannot behave as if they were following the complex rules of language, but only as if they were following simpler rules that can be described in terms of associations. Such rules reflect *statistical regularities* in a language – probabilities of one thing going with another.

Whether a machine has learned a statistical regularity or a more complex rule is not always an easy question to answer. David Rumelhart and Jay McClelland produced a connectionist machine that mimicked some aspects of how a child learns the past tense endings for English verbs. To a casual observer the behaviour of the machine was very impressive, and only a sophisticated analysis by Steven Pinker and Alan Prince showed that it did not know the detailed rules of the English past tense system. To simplify somewhat, it divided verbs into a number of subclasses and associated with each subclass the change required to produce the past tense from the present. Regular verbs, which follow the – ed rule, formed the largest group, other subgroups comprised irregular verbs that are similar to one another (e.g.

blow, grow, know, throw, in which the O sound is replaced by an E sound in the past tense). Any new verb was assimilated to one of those categories, sometimes with the wrong result. For example, it produced *grind,* rather than *ground,* as the past tense of *grind,* wrongly classifying it with verbs than do not change in the past tense, such as *beat, cut* and *hit.* And it produced *lended* instead of *lent* as the past tense of *lend,* wrongly treating that verb as regular. Learning by connectionist machines is discussed further in chapter 6.

FURTHER READING

Margaret Harris and Max Coltheart's *Language Processing in Children and Adults* (Routledge & Kegan Paul, 1986) is a good introduction to the psychology of language. My own *Psycholinguistics: Central Topics* (Methuen, 1985) is more advanced. For an interesting account of what it is like to teach a chimp to 'talk' see Herbert Terrace's *Nim: A Chimpanzee Who Learned Sign Language* (Eyre Methuen, 1980).

5   Thinking

The activities we call thinking are many and various. Sometimes 'thinking about' means little more than remembering or reminiscing. If I go into an electrical suppliers and ask for a part for an obscure make of washing machine, the man behind the counter might tell me that he doesn't have what I want and he'll have to 'think about' where one might be had. In all probability, he simply means that he cannot immediately remember where such a part can be obtained. In this sense 'thinking about' often signifies an extended mulling over that is likely to produce an affective response. I might, for example, be thinking about my trip to Vienna last year, rather than concentrating on (= 'thinking about' in a different sense) writing this chapter.

Although my electrical supplier might be trying to remember where he can get the part I want – thinking to himself 'where did I get one last time I wanted one?' – he might be engaged in everyday reasoning, which is more closely related to the concerns of this chapter than simple remembering. For example, he might be thinking: 'Fred prides himself on being able to mend any kind of washing machine, so he should know where to get the part. I know he's working at such-and-such a place today. If I telephone him there I can ask him.' This sort of reasoning is not particularly hard. Indeed, it is so straightforward we may not realise that it *is* reasoning. Nevertheless, cognitive scientists find everyday reasoning hard to study, for reasons that should be familiar from chapter 3. Everyday reasoning depends on knowledge about the world, knowledge of both generalities and specific facts stored in long-term memory, and there is, as yet, no good explanation of how we find the information we want so easily among all the facts we know. Cognitive scientists do, however, have an explanation for the other principal aspect of everyday reasoning: how the relevant bits of knowledge are used to solve the problem. People construct internal representations, called *mental models*, of the situation in the world they want to reason about and they change those models, in ways corresponding to ways the world can change, to try to find solutions to their problems. The mental models theory of reasoning makes three predictions about when reasoning will be difficult. First, since ordinary reasoning is linked to models of concrete situations, abstract reasoning should be difficult. Second, because the construction and development of models use information from long-term memory, reasoning should be harder when we cannot remember a pertinent bit of information or when we are confronted with a situation that our previous experience does not equip us to deal with. Third, people prefer to work with a single model, even though there may be many models that are compatible with the facts they are reasoning from, and many ways of developing a particular model. Conclusions that depend crucially on considering alternative models will be difficult to find.

Because everyday reasoning is difficult to study, these predictions have been tested by studying other kinds of thinking, most of them inherently more difficult than everyday problem solving: solving puzzles, including crossword puzzles, playing games such as chess, draughts and bridge, working on mathematical problems or proofs in logic, trying to find creative solutions to problems we haven't solved before. As this chapter will show, this research provides considerable support for the mental models theory.

PUZZLES

Why are puzzles so infuriating? They often seem simple, and yet are hard to solve. Puzzles are difficult because there are many ways of trying to solve them and often no obvious criterion for deciding which is best. This idea is illustrated by the well-known *8-puzzle* (see figure 5.1). The 8-puzzle comprises a square frame with eight numbers that can slide around a three

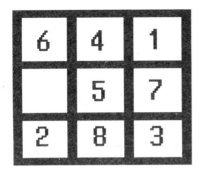 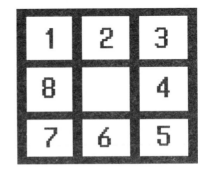

Figure 5.1 Examples of initial and final arrangements of the numbers 1 to 8 in the 8-puzzle

by three grid. These numbers must be moved via the vacant square until they are in a specified configuration.

Consider the starting position in figure 5.1. There are three possible first moves (slide the 2, the 5 or the 6 into the vacant square). Following each of these moves there are a number of further possibilities, though some simply get back to the starting position, and so on. At first glance there is nothing to choose between the three first moves, and simple multiplication shows that, if you always considered every possible move, the number of possibilities would soon get out of hand. Furthermore, the mental models theory predicts that considering more than one alternative development will be hard. Rubik's cube is a similar kind of puzzle, but with many more possibilities at each choice point. It is, therefore, very much more frustrating than the 8-puzzle, though there are systematic ways of trying to solve it, as the many books about it showed.

These considerations suggest one way of thinking about puzzles and their solutions and, hence, about the mental apparatus that underlies our puzzle-solving abilities, such as they are. This way of thinking about puzzles is called the *state-action* method. Using this method we characterise puzzles by the states they can be in and the actions that can be performed on them. For example, each state of the 8-puzzle is a possible configuration of the eight numbers, and the only possible action is to slide a number into an adjacent empty square. Given a particular starting state for the puzzle (e.g. the random configuration the manufacturers have meanly put it into) we can produce a *state-action tree*. This 'tree' is usually drawn upside down, with the starting state at the top. The tree then branches to each of the states that can be reached in one move from the starting state (three of them in the above example). It then branches again to the states that can be reached in two moves, and so on. In principle the tree can be extended for ever. Somewhere in the tree the *goal-state* will appear – in more than one place if there is more than one way of reaching it, as there is in the 8-puzzle. A solution to the problem is, therefore, a sequence of actions that gets from the starting state along the branches of the tree to the goal state.

Does the state-action method provide a good way of thinking about how people solve puzzles? The mental models theory suggests that people are unlikely to construct, in their minds, potentially infinite state-action trees. And clearly they do not. If they did, they would be able to read solutions to puzzles like the 8-puzzle from such trees directly. What has been suggested, however, is that people think of puzzles in terms of states and actions and, indeed, their subjective reports often suggest that they do. The question then arises, when people are deciding which action to perform, do they 'look ahead' in their mind's eye and see which sequence of actions gets them nearest to the goal state? To look ahead they would need to construct part of a state-action tree in their mind. The answer to this question is 'no', at least not in experimental studies in which people try to solve unfamiliar puzzles. They consider only the immediate possibilities and choose one of them. As the mental models theory predicts, developing alternatives in detail is difficult. However, seasoned puzzle book fans do not approach puzzles in this 'blind' way. Experts get around the limitation of only being able to develop one model in detail, perhaps because when they are highly familiar with a kind of problem they can devote more attention than is usual to considering alternative models. We will return to the question of 'looking ahead' by experts in the discussion of chess playing below.

The state-action method, in the form described above, is a 'brute force' or 'trial and error' method. Is there a better way of thinking about problems, or at least some problems? The answer is 'yes': divide and conquer! A disadvantage of the state-action method is that it does not divide up hard problems in a sensible way. Its concomitant advantage is that it can be used before a sensible way of dividing up a problem has been found.

The sensible way to tackle a problem that is too difficult to solve directly is to divide it into smaller problems that can be solved. If necessary, this division may take place in stages, with smaller problems being divided into yet smaller ones. Dividing problems into smaller problems is called *problem reduction*. A further advantage of this method is that it does not necessarily require the consideration of alternative models. Unfortunately, not all problems have straightforward reductions to simpler problems. Consider, for example, the Missionaries and Cannibals puzzle:

Missionaries and Cannibals: Transport three Missionaries and three Cannibals across a river in a boat that can only hold two people, but that needs at least one person to get it across the river. Cannibals must never outnumber Missionaries on either bank or the Missionaries will be eaten.

There is no obvious way of dividing the problem up into simpler problems. Furthermore, the solution is hard to find, because there are stages in the process, particularly at the end of the first line in figure 5.2, where one has to move from a state that seems quite close to the solution to one that seems further away.

The puzzle usually used to illustrate problem reduction is the Tower of Hanoi:

Tower of Hanoi: Three vertical pegs with four (or more) discs of decreasing size piled on one peg. Transfer the discs to the second peg by moving one disc at a time to another peg. Never place a larger disc on top of a smaller one.

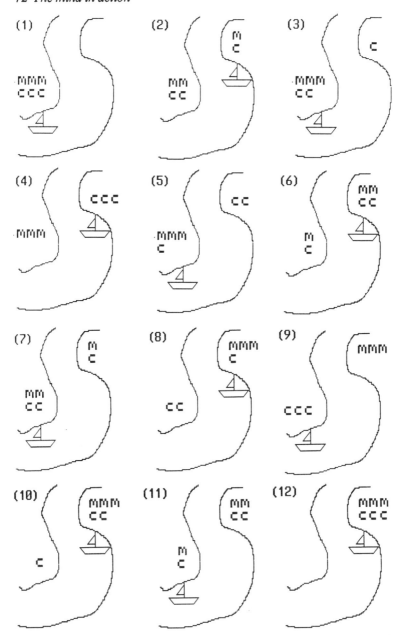

Figure 5.2 A sequence of eleven actions (linking twelve states) that solves the Missionaries and Cannibals problem. A letter 'm' represents one missionary and a 'c' one cannibal

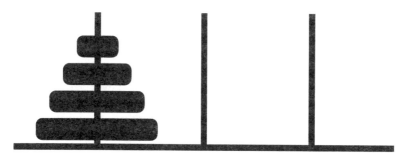

Figure 5.3 The Tower of Hanoi

The problem is illustrated in figure 5.3. You might like to think about how you would solve the problem, or about how you did solve it if you have ever played with a Tower of Hanoi, before you continue.

The Tower of Hanoi can, of course, be analysed using the state-action method. However, a more insightful solution is based on the observation that the problem can be divided into a series of problems similar to the original one, but simpler. To solve the four disc version, it is sufficient to solve the three disc version. The reason is straightforward. If you can move the top three discs onto the third peg, the large disc can then be moved onto the second peg, and the top three discs moved on top of it, using the same method used to move the three discs originally, but placing them on different pegs. Similarly, to solve the three disc problem you need to solve the two disc problem, and to solve the two disc problem you need to solve the trivial one disc problem. At each stage you also have to decide which peg to move the smallest disc onto first. (Answer: if you're moving an odd number of discs it should be the peg you want the pile to end up on, otherwise the other peg. Can you see why?)

Problem reduction is more powerful than the state-action method. The catch is that it is more difficult to apply – because it depends on finding a good analysis of the problem. Reduction of everyday problems usually depends on familiarity with the kind of problem one is faced with – that ubiquitous background knowledge again. Furthermore, although problem reduction does not require consideration of alternative models, it can impose considerable demands on memory by requiring complex elaboration of a single possibility, as the solution to the Tower of Hanoi illustrates.

GAMES

Games like chess might appear far removed from puzzle-book puzzles like Missionaries and Cannibals. However, a bit of thought (!) shows that a game of chess can be analysed in a similar way to Missionaries and Cannibals, using the state-action method. Each state is a configuration of the chess board and the actions that change one state to another are the moves that the players can make. The fact that a chess player has an adversary complicates matters slightly, but the same basic principles apply. Indeed, to emphasise the parallel, cognitive scientists refer to trying to win a game of chess or, more modestly, trying to decide on one's next move as *adversary problem solving*.

In our earlier discussion of the state-action method we introduced the idea of looking ahead in the state-action tree. Good chess players think through the consequences of a move before they make it. Are these two ideas related? The answer is 'yes', a sequence of moves that a chess player thinks through corresponds to a path through a state-action tree. The number of possible sequences of moves in a game of chess is frighteningly large, and chess players think through only a very small proportion of all the possible moves. They can cope with more than one development of the model representing the current state of the board, but not many more. Furthermore, chess players can only rarely think a sequence of moves through to a win, loss or stalemate. They must, therefore, have some means of evaluating the intermediate positions that they think through to, so that they can decide which they prefer. The positions that chess players prefer to think a sequence through to are so-called quiet positions, in which there is no imminent danger that a piece will be lost, other than in an exchange. The major consideration in evaluating such a position is the number of pieces left to each side, though other, strategic, considerations can also be important.

Since what is good for one player in a game of chess is bad for the other, players must assume that their opponents will always choose the move that is worst for them. This idea forms the basis of the *minimax procedure* used in computer chess-playing programs – players should *mini*mise the *max*imum loss that their opponents can inflict upon them. Minimax can, in principle, be used to decide among all possible moves or among a smaller set of moves initially selected by some other method. Chess-playing computer programs used to be like human chess players. They selected a small number of moves to follow up and then used minimax to analyse those moves in detail. Programs that run on small computers still work this way. However, computer chess is big business, and top programmers have available to them the most powerful machines in production. The most successful recent computer chess programs, which boast such names as BELLE and CRAY BLITZ, have reverted to the method of examining every possible position that can be reached in, say, the next five moves by each player. This method involves comparing hundreds of thousands of positions before deciding on each move. The very large number of operations that a modern computer can perform in a second – many millions of them – makes this sort of brute force method feasible. Unfortunately it provides few insights for cognitive scientists, since it bears no relation to the way that people solve difficult problems.

MATHEMATICS AND LOGIC

Some people solve puzzles or play chess for fun, others do mathematics. Indeed amateur mathematicians (or recreational mathematicians as they are usually called) often produce interesting new results or proofs. And most mathematics, whether we enjoy it or not, is a kind of problem solving. Fewer people entertain themselves with proofs in formal logic, but finding a logical proof is another example of problem solving. The study of how people prove theorems in mathematics and logic, like the study of human chess playing, shows that the state-action and problem reduction methods fail to account for many aspects of human thought.

At first one might ask: how can the state-action method be applied to mathematics and logic? What would be the states, for example? They would have to be something less tangible than the states of a chess board. One solution to this problem is to assume that a 'state' in a mathematical or logical proof is a set of statements that are given or have been proved so far, and that the actions are applications of the rules of mathematics to derive new statements. These states and actions are less concrete than those referred to in puzzles, so, as the mental models theory predicts, mathematical and logical reasoning is difficult. Is this state-action analysis plausible? If you have ever taken a course in formal logic, you will probably say 'yes'. In a logical proof you have a set of givens and a set of rules and you say 'well, I could either do this or this or this', which is similar to enumerating all the possible moves in Missionaries and Cannibals, or in a game of chess. Similarly, if you're trying to prove an algebraic equality, you know there are certain things you can do: multiply out expressions in brackets, regroup the items, and so on. So the idea of analysing theorem proving using the state-action method is not so bizarre as it first sounds.

Neither is it entirely frivolous. Many people have argued that all reasoning, or at least all correct reasoning, is the making of logical inferences. Indeed, it has been suggested that most inferences can be captured using a comparatively simple system of logic called *predicate calculus*. If much of our reasoning ability depends on a mental embodiment of predicate calculus, cognitive scientists need an account of how reasoning in predicate calculus might be mechanised, in the very general sense of mechanisation discussed in chapter 1.

Predicate calculus has a useful property called completeness, which not all systems of logic have. To say predicate calculus is complete is to say that there is a proof of every valid theorem in the system. This much has been known, in the abstract, for some time. But in the 1960s Allen Robinson devised the *resolution* method of theorem proving, which is particularly suitable for proving predicate calculus theorems by computer. Robinson did not make any psychological claims for the resolution method, and I certainly shall not, given that it depends on formal rules of inferences and not on the use of mental models. However, the resolution method shows that a mechanical method of making inferences in predicate calculus is possible in practice. We do not need to propose an unanalysable process of 'insight' to explain how people construct proofs in logic.

Resolution-based theorem provers work, but they do not prove very interesting theorems. They face two main problems. The first is that from any set of facts expressed in predicate calculus too many proofs can be produced. Finding the right one takes too long. Very fast modern computers can speed up resolution-based theorem proving but, because of the second problem, it is unlikely that the method will ever produce interesting proofs, no matter how fast it gets. The second problem is that, if you are trying to prove that a new fact follows from facts you already know, predicate calculus is not a good system to use. Logicians engage in technical 'in principle' arguments about what can and cannot be done in predicate calculus, but predicate calculus is not the way of everyday reasoning – rather mental models are – and it is not the way of real mathematics.

As in any academic discipline, mathematicians specialise. They work in selected areas of mathematics and they develop a feel for the methods that are appropriate in those areas. These methods are usually specific to a particular branch of mathematics and depend on its subject matter. The best known special method in mathematics is the use of diagrams in geometry. A diagram provides a single model of the information given – an external model rather than a mental one. In one sense, diagrams are unnecessary to geometric proofs, but no one would try to tackle such proofs without drawing diagrams. In principle, geometric proofs can be carried out using the resolution theorem proving method, with geometric problems represented in predicate calculus. But that method is inefficient, because it does not take advantage of the special features of the subject matter of geometry.

Although mathematical reasoning has its formal aspects, which make it difficult for many people, it is like everyday reasoning in that it makes use of specific knowledge about the domain in question. Indeed, almost all studies of human reasoning point to the use of domain-specific information

– background information that helps in the construction and development of appropriate mental models. People find all types of formal reasoning difficult: mathematics remains one of the least popular school subjects, psychology students struggle with statistics courses, formal logic is alien to most people. People are not very good, either, at a kind of reasoning called syllogistic reasoning, which was first studied by the ancient Greek philosopher Aristotle and which has been investigated extensively by cognitive scientists. A *syllogism* is an argument with two premises and a single conclusion that follows directly from them. Two examples are:

All As are Bs	All Bs are As
All Bs are Cs	No Cs are Bs
so, All As are Cs	so, Some As are not Cs

The premises and conclusion of a syllogism are always about some or all Xs being or not being Ys and the conclusion eliminates the term that is common to the two premises (B in the examples above), which is referred to as the *middle term*. Not all pairs of premises yield a valid conclusion.

Some syllogisms, like the first one above, are very easy, others, like the second, are very difficult. Phil Johnson-Laird has shown that the first syllogism can be solved using a single mental model, but the second requires the consideration of three separate models. When the information from the two premises is combined, there are three different ways of doing it, and the valid conclusion is the one that is true no matter which method of combination is selected. Choosing just one or two methods of combination is likely to suggest an invalid conclusion. As the models theory predicts, substituting concrete terms, such as artists, beekeepers, and chemists for the As, Bs, and Cs makes the problems easier, even when the terms are deliberately chosen so that the correct conclusions are not particularly plausible. Furthermore, having solved a concrete version of a syllogism does not help in solving a subsequent abstract version of the same syllogism. So the formal properties of syllogisms cannot be crucial in solving them. This fact is puzzling since, as Aristotle knew, there are straightforward formal procedures for deciding whether a syllogism is valid. These procedures, if applied systematically, produce more accurate results in syllogistic reasoning than people do.

Again these facts suggest that people do not reason by using formal rules. They are bad at syllogisms because they try to use their everyday reasoning abilities to solve them. Where possible, they use their knowledge of the world to build and manipulate mental models. This attempt to use background knowledge explains another well-documented fact about syllogistic reasoning. When asked to draw or evaluate a conclusion from two syllogistic premises, people are strongly influenced by whether the conclusion is plausible. Consider the following two parallel syllogisms, both of which are invalid:

> All of the Frenchmen are wine drinkers
> Some of the wine drinkers are gourmets
> so, Some of the Frenchmen are gourmets

> All of the Frenchmen are wine drinkers
> Some of the wine drinkers are Italians
> so, Some of the Frenchmen are Italians

The first is more likely to be assessed as valid than the second. The reason is that the implausibility of the conclusion in the second syllogism makes people realise that there can be two separate groups of wine drinkers, French and Italian. In the first version, the likelihood that some of the Frenchmen are gourmets leads people to overlook the parallel possibility, namely that there are two separate groups of wine drinkers, Frenchmen and gourmets. They fail to see that none of the Frenchmen need be gourmets. In fact, no valid syllogistic conclusion follows from either set of premises.

A formal method for checking the validity of syllogisms, such as Aristotle's, would not be influenced by plausibility, so the mental apparatus used in syllogistic reasoning by non-logicians cannot be based on purely formal procedures. The idea that people apply everyday reasoning abilities to problems for which those abilities are not particularly suited (syllogisms) explains why plausible conclusions are favoured, even when they are invalid. In everyday reasoning we expect to reach plausible conclusions most of the time. So, we are right to be suspicious of implausible conclusions and to be happy with plausible ones.

The difficulty people have with apparently simple formal reasoning problems, and the way that everyday content can make those problems simpler, is further demonstrated in the research of Peter Wason and his colleagues, who have studied a fascinating, and often frustrating set of reasoning problems. The best known of these problems is the *Wason selection task*.

Wason's Selection Task (Abstract Version): The following letters and numbers appear on the upper faces of four cards.

> E   K   2   7

Someone suggests that letters and numbers on the two faces of the cards conform to the following rule: if there is a vowel on one side, there is an even number on the other side. Which cards do you need to turn over to see if this rule correctly describes the four cards?

Before you read on, you should decide what you think the answer is, daunted by the fact that about 80 per cent of undergraduate students fail to solve the problem. The most common incorrect answer is E and 2, so if that was your answer you were wrong, but in good company. The choice of E is, of course, correct. If the E had an odd number on the back the rule would be incorrect. It is the choice of 2 that is wrong. You almost certainly did not pick the K card, since it is so clearly irrelevant. So, if the 2 has a consonant on the back it, too, is irrelevant. If it has a vowel on the back it is consistent with the rule, but it does not show the rule to be correct, since one of the other cards might not obey it. The 2 is, therefore, irrelevant, whatever is on the back of it. If the other cards obey the rule, it is true no matter what is on the back of the 2. Finding out what is there cannot help you to decide one way or the other. So, you need to turn the E, but not the K or the 2. What about the 7? Most people do not choose that card, but if it has a vowel on the back the rule is incorrect, whereas if it has a consonant the rule might still be true, if the other cards obey it. So, you do need to turn the 7, and the correct answer is to turn the E and the 7.

This abstract version of the selection task can only be solved using formal reasoning. People are not very good at formal reasoning, so they tend to get it wrong. There are a number of more concrete versions of the task. Wason himself devised the following:

> *Wason's Selection Task (Concrete Version):* Each of the cards in front of you represents a journey I have made, with the destination on one side and the method of transport on the other.
>
> Manchester   Leeds   Train   Car
>
> Someone suggests that my journeys conform to the following rule: whenever I go to Manchester, I go by train. Which cards do you need to turn over to see if this rule correctly describes my journeys?

With this version people more often chose the right cards. Presumably they realise that if the fourth card represented a car journey to Manchester, the rule would be incorrect. It seems, therefore, that in the concrete version of the selection task people bring relevant background knowledge to bear on the problem, as they would do in everyday reasoning. Their reasoning is, therefore, more accurate.

Two explanations have been proposed for how people try to solve the abstract version of the selection task. Wason's original idea was that people prefer to think about positive instances of rules rather than negatives ones. They are wrong to do so in the selection task because, the fact that one card conforms to the rule does not show that the others will, whereas a single card that does not conform to the rule shows that it is false. Many people have followed the philosopher of science, Karl Popper, in claiming that the only rational way to evaluate general statements (such as the rules in the selection task) is to try to show that they are false. No number of positive instances can guarantee that the next instance will not be negative, whereas one negative instance falsifies the generalisation once and for all. However, Popper ignores the fact that, for a hypothesis to be viable, there must be a range of positive cases it can explain. And we usually want to know whether a generalisation is viable before we bother to find out whether it is true or false.

The second kind of explanation for poor performance on the abstract version of the selection task is simpler. It says that when people find the logic of the problem too difficult, they choose cards whose top faces are explicitly mentioned in the rule (vowel and even number). This idea is discussed further in chapter 7, in relation to the explanations that people give for their choices.

An even more frustrating problem invented by Wason is the THOG problem:

> *THOG problem:* I have in mind a particular shape (either square or triangular) and a particular colour (either black or white). If any of the four figures shown in figure 5.4 has one, and only one, of these features that I have in mind it is called a THOG. Given that the black square is a THOG, what, if anything, can you say about whether each of the three remaining figures is a THOG?

Figure 5.4 The four geometrical shapes in the THOG problem

Again, you will probably want to try to solve this problem before you go on. The reason why the problem is difficult is because it contains both explicit and implicit or's, and, as the mental models theory emphasises, people are not very good at reasoning about alternatives. Furthermore, they are particularly bad when the alternatives are related only arbitrarily and not via background knowledge. THOG itself is a *disjunctive* concept. A THOG either has the colour that I have in mind (you don't know which it is) *or* the shape (again you don't know which it is) but not both. Very few ordinary language concepts have this property. The only clear examples in English are some of the less common kinship concepts. For example, a brother-in-law is either a sister's husband or a spouse's brother.

Another hidden disjunction ('or') quickly becomes apparent when you try to solve the THOG problem. Given that the black square is a THOG, what colour and shape do I have in mind? It must be either black and triangular or white and square, since a THOG has one and only one of the two features I am thinking of, but you cannot tell which. Therefore, to solve the problem, you must work systematically through the consequences of these two possibilities, which, according to the models theory, is difficult.

figure features	black square	white square	black triangle	white triangle
black and triangular	THOG	non-THOG (has neither feature)	non-THOG (has both features)	THOG (has one feature)
white and square	THOG	non-THOG (has both features)	non-THOG (has neither feature)	THOG (has one feature)

Thus, whichever of the two possible pairs of features I have in mind you can draw the same conclusion about which figures are THOGS and which are not. Indeed, you cannot tell from what I have told which shape and colour I am thinking of. With the THOG problem as with the selection task, the logic of the problem is clear when it is set out, but people find formal arguments about abstract content difficult.

One final problem invented by Wason is the 2–4–6 problem.

2–4–6 problem: I am thinking of a rule that describes sequences of three numbers. The sequence 2–4–6 obeys the rule. Ask me whether other sequences of numbers obey the rule. I will answer 'yes' or 'no'. Tell me the rule when you think you know what it is.

Unlike the selection task and the THOG problem, the 2–4–6 problem is not one you can solve on your own. But if I tell you the rule (any three numbers in increasing size) you can try it on your friends and see how they fare. What is interesting about the problem is not that people guess the wrong rule even when they're told to be very sure before they tell the experimenter, but how they set about checking their ideas. To investigate this matter, Wason asked people to write down each set of numbers they chose and the reason why they picked them. He found that they often fixed on a rule and then asked about sequences that conformed to it, just as, according to him, they pick cards in the selection task that could confirm the rule.

The *2–4–6* task is deliberately contrived so that people are likely to pick a more specific rule than the one the experimenter has in mind, for example numbers increasing in twos. The result is that every sequence that fits the specific rule also fits the general rule. So if a person picks positive instances of their rule the experimenter will say 'yes' even though the rule is wrong. This is another illustration of the fact that positive instances do not prove that a rule is correct. Other, as yet untested, instances may show the rule to be false. For example, a sequence such as 5–637–45948, which fits the experimenter's rule is a negative instance of the rule of numbers ascending in twos. If someone who thought that was the rule tested this sequence, they would discover their conjecture to be incorrect.

PROBABILISTIC REASONING

Everyday reasoning is often based on probabilities rather than certainties, yet people have difficulty taking proper account of probabilities. Consider the following problem:

> Richard is muscular, fit and can run 100 metres in twelve seconds. Do you think it more likely that he is a librarian or a librarian interested in outdoor sports?

Many people choose the second alternative, even though Richard cannot be a librarian interested in outdoor sports unless he is a librarian. A second problem further illustrates how counterintuitive the solutions to problems involving probabilities can be.

> Eighty-five per cent of the taxis in a particular city are green and the rest are blue. A witness identifies a cab involved in an accident as blue. Under tests the witness correctly identifies both blue and green cabs on four out of five occasions. What is the probability that the cab was in fact blue?

The answer is:

$$\frac{0.15 \times 0.8}{0.85 \times 0.2 + 0.15 \times 0.8} = 0.41$$

Surprisingly it is *more* likely that the taxi was *green*, even though the witness said it was blue. The correct answer, unlike human reasoners, is strongly influenced by the high proportion of green taxis.

Daniel Kahneman and Amos Tversky have suggested that people get the answers to such problems wrong for the same reason that they get other kinds of problems wrong. They do not naturally use the formal rules of reasoning – in this case those of mathematics – that would produce the correct solutions. Instead, they use rules of thumb, such as *representativeness* and *availability*.

Kahneman and Tversky's formulation of these rules is a small step towards solving the difficult problem of explaining how relevant information is extracted from long-term memory for use in thinking and reasoning. Representativeness is the rule that makes us think Richard is a librarian interested in outdoor sports. He is not representative of librarians in general, but he *is* representative of librarians interested in outdoor sports. Availability says: estimate the likelihood of something by how readily examples of it come to mind. This rule explains why, for example, people tend to overestimate the proportion of the population that dies in air crashes, which is actually very small. They can readily bring examples of plane crashes to mind, since such disasters are widely publicised.

EXPERTS AND EXPERT SYSTEMS

So far, except in the case of chess, we have discussed the kind of reasoning that anyone might engage in. But, particularly in advanced societies, we employ a principle of the division of mental as well as of manual labour. We have experts in various fields. Human experts are expensive both to train and to employ, and developing countries in particular would benefit if human expertise could be automated and reproduced cheaply in the form of computer programs. This idea has led AI researchers to develop so-called *expert systems*.

Expert systems are important because they promise to be the first major application of AI research. They also have potential theoretical importance – building them should help us understand how human experts reason. Those expert systems that have been most successful have taken many man-years to build. These systems include DENDRAL and XCON. DENDRAL helps organic chemists to establish the structure of complex molecules. Several papers published in academic journals have reported work in which DENDRAL has been used. XCON decides how the parts of expensive bespoke computer systems should be put together. It is reputed to have saved the computer manufacturer Digital Equipment Corporation (DEC) large sums of money. More controversial are programs that carry out medical diagnoses, the most famous of which is MYCIN, a program that diagnoses serious bacterial infections and suggests courses of treatment. Doctors are reluctant to rely on such programs while there is a possibility that they will make mistakes, for both moral and legal reasons.

As we saw in the discussion of chess, what differentiates experts from novices is mastery of a body of knowledge that people do not typically have. Experts can, therefore, devote their cognitive resources to reasoning from that body of knowledge. Three important problems have to be solved in the construction of expert systems. The most important is to determine what knowledge human experts have. Unfortunately, finding out is not simply a matter of asking the experts. Often they cannot make explicit all of the knowledge they use. An extensive survey of how experts work may have to be carried out. The second problem is how to encode experts' knowledge into a computer program. The third is how to deal with probabilistic evidence. For example, a patient's symptoms do not provide unequivocal evidence for a particular diagnosis, but may be compatible with several, with different symptoms suggesting one diagnosis more strongly than another. How should the various sources of information be combined to produce a single diagnosis and suggest a course of treatment? Again, experts find it difficult to make explicit how they accomplish this task. Many expert systems use techniques derived from the mathematical theory of probability. Others use specially devised techniques.

CREATIVITY

One aspect of thought that we have not yet discussed is creativity, which is important in both science and technology and in the arts. Solutions to everyday problems may also be creative. By its nature, creative thought is difficult to study experimentally. You cannot bring a group of people into a laboratory and force them to be creative. Nevertheless, there are ways of studying creativity and there are important questions about creative thought that are studied in cognitive science. The most important of these is: what are the mechanisms that underlie such thought? In particular, is creative thinking like ordinary thinking? Is it, for example, based on the use of mental models? If it is not like ordinary thinking, how does it differ?

The consensus view is that creativity does not require any special kind of thought process that is not part of more mundane kinds of thinking. One point in favour of this view is that it is parsimonious. It would be difficult to explain why a small number of individuals think in a different way from everyone else. The view is also consistent with the fact that whether a particular idea counts as creative – or how creative it appears – depends on its context, not just on the idea itself. A creative solution may bring knowledge to bear on a problem that was not previously thought to be relevant. And it may model an aspect of the world in a new way – the structure of the benzene molecule as a ring, to take a simple example. However, once that knowledge has been brought to bear, or that new type of model created, it will be easier for similar solutions to emerge for related problems, though they will be less creative. Creative thinking is likely to be more complex than other kinds of thinking, to depend on ideas or combinations of ideas that are surprising or implausible from a previous perspective. But as far as the mental processes that produce creative thoughts are concerned, cognitive science regards them as more of the same rather than something extraordinary.

FURTHER READING

The mental models theory of thinking and reasoning is described in detail in Phil Johnson-Laird's *Mental Models* (Cambridge University Press, 1983). Jonathan Evans discusses how and why our thinking can go wrong in his *Biases in Human Reasoning* (Lawrence Erlbaum Associates, 1989). David Perkins' book *The Mind's Best Work* (Harvard University Press, 1981) argues that creative thinking is not qualitatively different from other kinds of thinking.

6 Learning

'You learn something new every day.' Perhaps this saying is British and reflects the British penchant for understatement. Anyone who reads a newspaper or listens to the news on the radio absorbs a considerable amount of new information from that source alone. But it is not just facts that we learn. We learn how to do things: how to play tennis, or to play the piano, how to play them better, how to ride a bike, how to use an espresso coffee machine, a word processor, an electric knife sharpener. And how do we learn? In a variety of ways. Some things, such as parts in amateur dramatics, we learn by rote. Others, primarily facts, we are simply told – by our friends, by our adversaries, by journalists. We learn by our mistakes, we learn from examples and, particularly in the case of skills, we learn by practice, practice and more practice.

These facts about learning raise a host of questions for cognitive science. What, if anything, do different kinds of learning have in common? How, in cognitive terms, can we characterise the process (or processes) of learning? What does a person have to know, or what abilities do they need, to learn something? Which of the things we know do we *not* have to learn and how did we come to know them? In this chapter we will consider these questions and others about the comparatively neglected topic of learning.

It is not long since learning theory was one of the principal branches of psychology. From the 1920s through to the 1950s – the heyday of behaviourism – a large proportion of psychologists studied learning. Now learning is an unfashionable area for research. In AI, too, learning by machines has been a neglected topic, though one frequently hears the claim that machines will never be really intelligent until they can learn. Similarly, no one would deny the importance of learning for human cognition. True, some of our cognitive abilities are built-in, and their development can be explained in terms of maturation rather than learning. Yet so much of what we know, and so many of the things we can do, we have to learn.

The question of how we learn things – how we find out about the world – is one that has puzzled philosophers for centuries. Indeed, psychological work on learning has been influenced, perhaps more than many psychologists realise, by the controversy between rationalism and empiricism, which dominated philosophical debate from René Descartes (1596–1650) to Immanuel Kant (1724–1804) and which continues to the present day. Rationalists claim we are born knowing much of what we know – we do not learn it from experience. There are two major problems for this doctrine: what is the source of the knowledge that is built into us, and what guarantees it *is* knowledge, rather than misinformation? In one sense the theory of evolution has suggested answers to these questions. People and animals whose behaviour accurately reflects what the world is like are more likely to survive than ones that behave on the basis of incorrect information. And often it is safer for an animal to rely on built-in information than to learn something – it may be dead before it does. These answers are, of course, not the kind of answers that rationalist philosophers were looking for.

Empiricists claim that all knowledge is acquired. The mind of a new born child is blank – it is a *tabula rasa* (blank slate). Knowledge takes the form of *associations* between *ideas*. Indeed, the form of empiricism that was particularly influential in experimental psychology is known as *associationism*. Ideas enter the mind via the senses. Associations are formed as a result of the experience of things going together in the world. The more often things are experienced together, the more strongly the ideas corresponding to them are associated. The principal problem with the idea that all knowledge takes the form of associations is that much of our knowledge, for example the knowledge of language discussed in chapter 4, has a structure that is too complex to be described in terms of associations.

Associationism underlies all the forms of behaviourism that dominated experimental psychology in the Anglo-Saxon world from the early years of this century to the 1950s. In its more extreme forms, such as those of John B. Watson, the founder of behaviourism, and B. F. Skinner, one of its most vociferous and controversial proponents, the mentalistic vocabulary of ideas in the mind disappears and is replaced by talk of associations between stimuli (in the world) and the responses of animals to them. Nevertheless, these forms of behaviourism retain the assumption that what an animal learns can be characterised as associations of varying strengths. For example, in a simple T-maze experiment, in which a rat has to run along the 'vertical' part of the T and learn to turn left (say) to get food, the rat forms an association between seeing the junction (stimulus) and deciding to turn left (response). The strength of the learned association will depend on factors such as how hungry the animal is and how reliably it finds food in the left arm of the maze.

Behaviourists studied learning in rats and pigeons, primarily. They took from empiricism the idea that the mind of a newborn animal is a *tabula rasa* and made the additional assumption that the *laws of learning* are universal – they are the same for all species. So laws discovered by studying rats and pigeons, which are very easy to keep as laboratory animals, should generalise to humans, which are not!

The amount of research generated by behaviourists was enormous. They identified two major types of learning, *classical conditioning* and *instrumental conditioning*. Classical conditioning is exemplified in the famous studies by the Russian physiologist Ivan Pavlov, who showed that dogs would learn to salivate to the sound of a bell, after the bell had become associated with the subsequent presentation to the dog of a piece of meat. Instrumental conditioning is exemplified by behaviour in the Skinner box, named after B. F. Skinner. In instrumental learning an animal learns to associate a voluntary behaviour, such as pressing a lever, with a 'reward' or 'punishment', say the appearance of food in a hopper on the side of the box – it learns that its action is instrumental in producing food. Depending on whether the result of the action is good (food for a hungry animal) or bad (electric shock) the frequency of lever pressing (or other voluntary behaviour) will increase or decrease accordingly.

What did psychologists find out about learning from these studies? Many of their findings were, not surprisingly, technical. Some, however, are easily understood. One of the best known is the effect of 'partial reinforcement' on 'extinction'. Partial reinforcement means, for example, that an animal does not get food every time it presses the bar, but only sometimes. Extinction is what happens when we stop giving the food. It is so called because we expect the animal to stop pressing the bar. An animal that is given food every time it presses the bar quickly stops pressing when its reward is withdrawn. One given food only sometimes continues to press for longer. Intuitively the reason is that the animal is not surprised when some presses do not produce food. That is what it has been led to expect.

With hindsight the behaviourist assumptions of a *tabula rasa* and universal laws of learning are implausible. Ethologists, starting with Konrad Lorenz and Niko Tinbergen, identified innate behaviours that differ from species to species. The most well-known of them centre around the phenomenon of imprinting. A newborn gosling, for example, follows the first large moving object it encounters, and treats it as its mother. Normally the 'object' *is* its mother, and all is well. However, when Lorenz was the first thing seen by a brood of goslings, he was forced to become their stepmother. Imprinting raises problems for both of the assumptions mentioned above. Since it happens immediately after birth, the mind of a newborn gosling cannot be a *tabula rasa*. At the very least, it contains the information that the gosling should follow the first large moving object it sees. The fact that young of different species imprint on things with different characteristics and that some do not imprint at all casts doubt on the idea of universal laws of learning.

Another problem for the idea of a *tabula rasa* is the complexity of some of the things that people learn. In particular, many people believe that the complexities of the rules governing our use of language cannot be characterised in terms of associations however intricate those associations might be. So, assuming that much of what rats and pigeons learn *can* be characterised in terms of associations, the laws that govern learning by rats and pigeons are unlikely to describe the way we learn language.

B. F. Skinner tried to counter this view in his book *Verbal Behavior*, in which he attempted to explain how ideas from learning theory could be applied to language learning. However, the book was not based on systematically collected empirical evidence about how children learn language. It was almost entirely impressionistic. Noam Chomsky argued that the impressionistic nature of Skinner's case masked its fundamental inadequacy. As a result of his critique, published in 1959, behaviourist approaches to human learning vanished almost overnight, and the cognitive era began. One of the more controversial of Chomsky's own views is that our ability to learn languages depends on an innate store of knowledge – Chomsky is a confessed rationalist.

No cognitive scientist can embrace empiricism as propounded by the British empiricist philosophers John Locke (1632–1704) and David Hume (1711–76) and their followers, or as it manifested itself in behaviourism. There are two main reasons why they cannot. First, as we have already said, much of what we know does not take the form of associations and cannot be learned from observing what events, states and processes are found together in the world. Second, cognitive scientists focus on mental processes, which were largely ignored by associationists of both the philosophical and psychological varieties. But mental processes are required to learn even simple associations. The mind must have some structure. It cannot be completely blank.

WHY EARLY COGNITIVISTS IGNORED LEARNING

Associationism may not be the correct account of how people learn things, but learning is a psychological fact, and cognitive scientists have a duty to try to explain it. One might, therefore, ask why it has been neglected in both cognitive psychology and, more particularly, AI. Although there is more psychological work on learning than is at first apparent – hidden under heads such as skill acquisition – its relative neglect is largely explained by a fundamental assumption of the cognitive approach to higher mental functions. This assumption is that cognitive processes can be characterised as computations, in a very general sense of that term – as examples of information processing. In the early days of AI it was argued that there is, therefore, no fundamental difference between the way a person solves a problem, say, and the way a machine does. Although machines and brains are made of different kinds of stuff – neurons and electronic components, respectively – they can carry out the same information processing operations. It does not matter that the person learned to solve problems and the machine was programmed to do so. Problem solving can be studied without worrying about how the problem solver acquired its skill.

In the 1950s it was as well that this assumption made sense, since people could write programs that solved problems or played chess, at least in a limited way, but they could not write programs that learned these tasks. An important program written by Arthur Samuel learned to play the simpler game of chequers (draughts). And a quite different kind of program, the perceptron – forerunner of the connectionist machines discussed later in this chapter – learned to classify simple visual patterns. But in general the problem of learning was regarded as too difficult for AI researchers to address.

Samuel's chequer program can learn in two ways. The less interesting of the two is simple rote learning. We saw in the last chapter that game-playing programs look ahead to upcoming positions and decide which of the ones they can reach they like best. In its rote learning mode Samuel's program stores a value for each position it encounters. These values are easier to retrieve from memory than to recompute. So, in a fixed amount of time, the program can evaluate more continuations.

Samuel called the program's second method of learning *learning by generalisation*. When using this method the program compares evaluations of positions made during a game with the real values of those positions, as determined by the way the game turned out. Any discrepancies are used to change the way positions are evaluated. The details of the method are complex. The method itself is important because it is an example of a common phenomenon in learning – generalisation. In this case the program generalises from evaluations of specific positions to (what it 'hopes' is) a good method for evaluating *any* board position.

Two cases of learning by generalisation merit further consideration. One is learning the meanings of words. One might be tempted to say: word meanings are learned from definitions. But people do not learn most of the words they know from explicit dictionary definitions (think how many dictionary definitions are useless, those of colour words, for example, or the names of common animals). We learn the meaning of words from examples, perhaps only a few examples – our powers of generalisation are great. When children learn words they often overgeneralise. Most of us have known children who used the word 'dog' (often pronounced 'goggie') to refer to all kinds of animal. Melissa Bowerman reports a more striking example. Between 16 months and two years her daughter Eva used the word *moon* to refer to the moon itself, to slices of lemon, to cows' horns, to a crescent-shaped piece of paper, to a shiny green leaf and to pictures of vegetables.

The other kind of generalisation is learning a rule or law or general fact from situations or happenings that are instances of it. Many kinds of learning fall under this head: for example, learning how the physical world works, learning how people behave, and learning the rules of language (see chapter 4). This kind of learning is similar to the discovery of scientific laws by a process that philosophers of science call induction. The problem about induction is that generalisations must be induced from a limited number of observations. But just as infinitely many lines can be drawn through a fixed number of points on a sheet of graph paper, infinitely many generalisations are compatible with a limited set of observations. This 'graph paper' analogy illustrates another point. Most of the lines will be complex curves. A few – with luck just one – will be simple, perhaps a straight line or a neat curve. This line is the one of interest. Similarly, most of the generalisations compatible with a set of observations will be complicated and uninteresting. Some will be relatively simple and often the simplest generalisation is more or less correct. The moral is that learning mechanisms should not just choose a generalisation compatible with the observations they make. They must be biased to choose simple generalisations. Unfortunately simplicity is not always as easy to define as it is in the case of lines on graph paper.

LEARNING BY CONNECTIONIST MACHINES

Over the last few years a new kind of model of the mind, the *connectionist* or *parallel distributed processing* models that we mentioned in chapter 1, have assumed increasing importance. Many of these models learn to perform tasks rather than being programmed to carry them out. And although proponents of connectionism do not claim that the specific learning methods they have developed are used in the brain, they make general claims about the psychological relevance of the way these machines learn.

As outlined in chapter 1, a connectionist machine has a (usually large) number of simple *units*, which resemble the nerve cells, or neurons, of the brain. Each unit has a level of activation, which it transmits to units connected to it. The connections between the units have numbers called *weights* attached to them, which determine how much activation is passed. The units are organised in layers, most typically three: an input layer, an intermediate (or hidden) layer, and an output layer. Units in the input layer are activated by external *stimuli*. The nature of these stimuli depends on what aspect of cognition the connectionist machine is supposed to model. For example, if it is a model of the visual system the input will be a visual pattern and the activation in the input layer a representation of that pattern. The input units then correspond to the receptor cells of the retina. In a connectionist machine that modelled the learning of general concepts, such as cat or dog, from instances of them, the input would represent features of cats or dogs that are important for classifying them as such. For example, there might be an input unit that was highly activated if the input barked and not activated if it did not. In testing such a model, the inputs must be coded for the computer. At present such a machine is not expected to learn about cats and dogs by observing them, only by being given representations of examples of them.

Once the input units have been activated, they pass their activation, via the weighted connections, to the hidden units, which in turn pass activation to the output units. Activation in the output units represents the machine's response to the stimulus. Depending on what the machine does, the number of output units may be large or small. For a simple classification task one output unit may suffice. High activation in that unit means 'yes' (it is a dog, for example), low activation means 'no' (it isn't). The more possible responses, the more output units will be needed – different responses are coded by different patterns of activation rather than by different levels of activation in a single unit. Figure 1.3 (see p. 17) is a schematic diagram of a connectionist machine.

So far we have described a connectionist machine performing a task, not one learning how to perform it. There are several ways in which connectionist machines can learn. The most important is a method of *supervised* learning known as *backwards error propagation using the generalised delta rule* (back propagation, for short). Supervised learning is learning that requires a teacher. The generalised delta rule is a way of using the feedback that the teacher provides. A connectionist machine that learns by this rule starts with the weights on its connections set to random values. It is given an input and allowed to produce a pattern of activation in its output units. This pattern will almost certainly represent an incorrect response to the input, so the teacher tells the machine what pattern of activation it should have produced. The delta rule is then used to adjust the weights, so that if the machine were given the same stimulus again its output would be more like the intended output. The difference between the machine's actual response and the correct one is the 'error'. The term 'back propagation' refers to the fact that the method of adjusting the weights starts at the output layer and works backwards through the hidden layer to the input layer. This process is repeated for more (usually many more) sample inputs.

In back propagation the weights are not adjusted so that the machine would give the right output for the input it has just seen. That could drastically change its response to other inputs. The rule is formulated so that the error generated by the most recent input has a comparatively small effect. For this reason the adjustment of the weights can be very slow and a connectionist machine can take a long time to learn using the generalised delta rule. The goal of learning by back propagation is not to adjust the weights so that the machine gives the right output for all the inputs in the sample it learns from. It is, more ambitiously, to select weights that will give the right output for any input. Indeed, when the learning is over, the machine should be tested using new inputs that were not in the learning sample.

Connectionist machines can learn to perform more difficult tasks than an earlier kind of network model, the *perceptron*, whose limitations were documented by Marvin Minsky and Seymour Papert in the late 1960s. Nevertheless, the weighted connections of a connectionist machine encode associations of different strengths, so connectionism is a version of associationism and, as such, subject to the problems of previous versions of that doctrine. Despite this fact, connectionist machines have been constructed that allegedly carry out the complex information processing tasks that are part of language use, thinking and problem solving. Rumelhart and McClelland's English past tense learning machine, discussed in chapter 4, is one example. The claims made for this particular machine were, perhaps, overzealous. However, it remains to be seen whether further developments in connectionist modelling can overcome the limitations of its fundamentally associationist approach, and to what extent such developments will retain the associationist assumptions of current connectionist models.

LEARNING IN AI

Learning by connectionist machines contrasts sharply with the work on learning in traditional AI, much of which is of only marginal relevance to cognitive science. One of the best known AI learning programs was written by Patrick Winston at the Massachusetts Institute of Technology, perhaps the leading centre of AI research in the late 1960s and early 1970s. Winston's program inhabits the BLOCKSWORLD (see chapters 1 and 2). It is supplied with simple BLOCKSWORLD concepts, such as PILLAR and LINTEL, and learns slightly more complex concepts such as ARCH. However, these concepts are defined structurally (an ARCH is a LINTEL supported by two separated PILLARS). No reference is made, for example, to the reasons why people build arches. Furthermore, Winston's program provides no answer to the question of how concepts such as LINTEL and PILLAR are learned.

Winston's program embodies two ideas that are interesting in themselves, though it does not use them in a fully general form. First, the program learns a concept from positive examples and *near misses*. Near misses are like exemplars of the concept the program is trying to learn, but each near miss differs from a real example in one important respect. So a near miss ARCH might have a LINTEL supported by two PILLARS, but with the PILLARS touching. Using what it knows so far, together with the fact that this structure is not an ARCH, the program can work out that the PILLARS of an ARCH must not touch. It cannot learn anything from being told that something very different from an ARCH is not an ARCH.

The second idea embodied in the program is that to learn a concept you need to know other concepts. This idea is a special case of the notion that a blank mind cannot learn anything. As we saw in the argument against associationism, all learning requires some cognitive ability, and part of what it is to have an ability is to know something. We will return to the question of whether any concepts must be innate at the end of this chapter.

Winston called the procedures in his program that construct general concepts from information about specific instances *induction heuristics*. The idea of an induction heuristic has been generalised and made more sophisticated in recent work in the field that has come to be known as *machine learning*. In particular, Ryszard Michalski has written a series of complex induction programs that have found applications, albeit rather specialised ones, in the real world (e.g. discrimination between soybean plants with different diseases). However, these programs do not operate the way people do, and they tell us little about human learning. A serious limitation on them, as a contribution to cognitive science, is that they have to formulate generalisations using the same descriptive terms that they use to classify the instances, by combining them with logical connectives, such as *and* and *or* to produce more complex descriptive terms. So if an induction heuristic is given information about the following animals, it will conclude that what they have in common is that they are all grey mice. Each is grey *and* each is a mouse.

creature 1: small, grey, mouse
creature 2: large, three-legged, grey, mouse
creature 3: small, tail-less, grey, mouse
creature 4: grey, mouse

General concepts constructed in this way from simpler concepts are quite unlike ordinary language concepts.

Two other AI learning programs are worth mentioning. The first, written by Gerald Sussman, learns how to make plans for stacking and unstacking blocks in the BLOCKSWORLD. Sussman called the program HACKER because it writes its plans in a programming language called CONNIVER, and in the early 1970s a hacker was a person who spent all his or her time programming. Since then it has come to refer to a person who gains unauthorised access to a computer system. Like Winston's program, HACKER needs a teacher and it learns only when it can nearly solve the problem it is set. It is the teacher's responsibility to present HACKER with a series of problems of gradually increasing difficulty.

The second program is Doug Lenat's controversial Automated Mathematician (AM). This program starts with some basic concepts from a branch of mathematics known as set theory. Set theory is one of the most fundamental parts of mathematics. For example, mathematicians define basic arithmetical concepts, such as positive whole number, in terms of sets. AM has rules for making new concepts from the ones it already knows, and for making conjectures about them. For example, Lenat intended that AM should discover the concept of a positive whole number, and it did. Another concept it discovered was that of a prime number. AM does not prove the conjectures it makes, but it does produce interesting ones. For example, it proposed the so-called fundamental theorem of arithmetic – that every number can be expressed as the product of a series of prime numbers (e.g. $17 = 1 \times 17$, $32 = 2 \times 2 \times 2 \times 2 \times 2$, $63 = 3 \times 3 \times 7$ etc.). AM illustrates the idea of learning by exploration, though its own explorations are somewhat different from those of a human mathematician.

I will conclude this section on learning in AI by mentioning a quite different line of research, that on *computer-aided learning* or *intelligent tutoring systems*. This work provides indirect information about how people learn. It does so by studying, and attempting to automate, ways in which they can be taught. One of the early advocates of computer-aided instruction was B. F. Skinner, who devised a tutoring method in which a computer presented questions to students and recorded their answers. If the answers were incorrect, the computer presented more questions on the same topic, until the student was deemed to have mastered it. It then proceeded to the next topic. Skinner assumed that getting the answer right was sufficient 'reward' to make the students learn. And in line with his behaviourist principles, his programs made no assumptions about the mental processes of the students.

More recent *intelligent* tutoring systems take the cognitive processes of learners seriously. These systems have three principal components: a knowledge base, a model of the student, and a set of teaching strategies. The knowledge base contains the information that is to be imparted to the student. But it can also be used to generate explanations of why answers to particular questions are correct. Intelligent tutoring systems do not simply tell students when they are wrong, they try to use teaching methods that make them realise why they are wrong. The model of the student is particularly important here.

In particular the system needs to know what misconceptions students are likely to have, and what methods of solving problems they use. As far as *teaching* methods are concerned, the easiest is probably to evaluate students' solutions to problems directly. However, there is some evidence that less direct methods of tutoring are more effective, though they are harder to implement in a computer system. For example, if an intelligent tutoring system can identify a particular misconception that a student has, it might try to make the student discover the misconception for themselves by devising a problem in which the role of the misconception in producing the wrong answer is readily apparent.

WHAT CONCEPTS ARE INNATE?

A special case of the question, which we discussed at the beginning of this chapter, of what is learned and what is innate, is whether any of our concepts are innate. We characterised empiricists as claiming that everything is learned. In fact, that characterisation is misleading. Empiricists typically endorse the doctrine, which can be traced back through Thomas Aquinas to Aristotle, that nothing can be in the mind except what is first in the senses. Sensory concepts (red, blue, green, yellow; loud, quiet; sweet, salty, etc.) are innate or, at least, they are automatically available to people who have the relevant experiences. All other concepts are built from sensory ones by the process of association, according to the empiricists. The philosopher Jerry Fodor has argued against this view and concluded that all concepts are innate. He claims that if non-sensory concepts were constructed from sensory ones by the process of association, there should be exact definitions for non-sensory concepts. However, according to Fodor, there are very few satisfactory definitions. So non-sensory concepts are not built out of sensory ones, their definitions cannot be learned from those of sensory concepts, and they must be innate. This idea at first seems absurd. If all concepts have to be innate, every concept that anyone will ever use must be built into all of us. Did everyone born before 1975 have the concept of a yuppie? And, if they did, why did they never use it?

Fodor's counter to this riposte is that all concepts, including sensory ones, have to be activated by *triggering experiences*. Congenitally blind people never have triggering experiences for colour concepts and so they never acquire them. Similarly, Fodor argues, people who do not have the experiences that trigger the concept of a yuppie – those who lived in the pre-yuppie era, for example – will not acquire that concept. Fodor's argument is a challenging one, but it is not conclusive. It has two major weaknesses. The first is that being blind because of damage to one's visual system is a different kind of deficit from not having encountered a yuppie, yet both count as not having had the relevant triggering experiences, according to Fodor. The second is that Fodor's criteria for a good definition are unrealistic. Dictionary makers would be reluctant to agree with his conclusion that there are hardly any good definitions. Nevertheless, Fodor has forced cognitive scientists to think more clearly about what must be innate if concepts are to be learned.

FURTHER READING

Tony Dickinson's *Contemporary Animal Learning Theory* (Cambridge University Press, 1980) provides an introduction to the technicalities of recent psychological work on animal learning. John Pearce's *An Introduction to Animal Cognition* (Lawrence Erlbaum Associates, 1987) covers a wider range of topics.

7 Action

Sometimes we sit and think; sometimes we stand and take in a magnificent view. But if cognition does not always lead directly to action, the two are intimately linked, sometimes in ways that are not immediately obvious. For example, the philosopher J. L. Austin had to draw attention to what is, with hindsight, an obvious fact: by saying the right thing in the right context we are often performing an action. The examples are commonplace: 'I bet you £10', 'I promise I'll be there', 'I name this ship the *Cutty Sark*', 'I do' (in a marriage ceremony).

Saying something is sometimes an action, but it is not a prototypical action. Prototypical actions involve bodily movements. We can move our bodies because they are jointed and because we have muscles to move the jointed parts. The anatomy of the human body is well understood, and in recent years much has been learned about how muscles work. A muscle can contract but it cannot extend itself. It can only be extended if it is relaxed and is pulled out (usually by another muscle). For this reason muscles work in agonist/antagonist pairs. For example, we can bend our arms at the elbow by contracting the muscle in the upper arm known as the biceps. To straighten it up again we have to use a different muscle, the triceps, to pull it back into place. Fortunately, antagonistic pairs of muscles do not contract together, otherwise we might have sore joints or even broken bones.

Muscles are made of fibres, which are made to contract by nerve impulses from the brain. Among the fibres are structures called *muscle spindles*, which monitor the tension in the muscle, and prevent joints from moving when they are supposed to be still. When there is movement about a joint, the brain must, therefore, not only tell the muscle fibres to contract, it must also tell the muscle spindles how tense the muscle should be in its new position. The spindles can then exert fine control in bringing the body to its new position. If a muscle encounters an unexpected resistance, the spindles tell it to contract more. Indeed they can tell it to contract more and more powerfully, again putting our bones and tendons in jeopardy if the movement we want to make

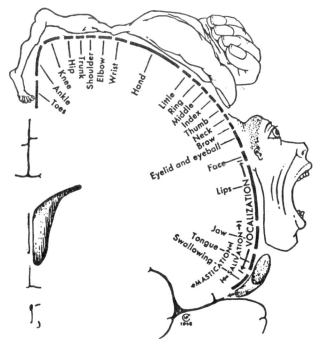

Figure 7.1 The organisation of the motor cortex. The area next to each part of the figure is devoted to controlling the corresponding part of (the opposite side of) the body

is obstructed by an immovable object. The overall tension in a muscle is therefore monitored by further structures known as *Golgi tendon organs*, which prevent muscular tension from becoming too high.

The skeletal muscles that produce bodily movements are controlled by the motor cortex, a band of the cortex – the outer layer of the brain – that runs across the top of the head in front of the ears. The motor cortex is arranged *topographically* – parts of the motor cortex that are close together control muscles that are near one another in the body. This organisation is illustrated graphically in figure 7.1. The parts of the figure are drawn next to the parts of the cortex that control them. The figure is distorted because the amount of motor cortex devoted to an area of the body depends not on its size but, roughly speaking, on its importance. The hands and face get more than their fair share, the trunk much less. A further complication is that the right side of the brain controls the left side of the body and vice versa.

The anatomy and physiology of movement are more complex than this brief sketch indicates, but we must turn to other questions. Much of the psychological research on movement has investigated physical, rather than cognitive, characteristics of movements. One important question is which movements are ballistic and which are controlled by feedback. A ballistic movement is planned in advance, and executed by a single command to the muscles. What happens during the action does not influence its execution. So, if an object unexpectedly gets in the path of a ballistic arm movement, the arm will hit the object and it may be injured. Deliberate movements are not usually ballistic. For example, you might plan to move a glass from a table to a chair. If you thought the glass was plastic but it was really made of glass, it would move downward more quickly than you anticipated. However, you would be able to take account of what happened and adjust the force you were applying accordingly. Some bodily movements, for example the small movements of our eyes, known as *saccades*, have traditionally been characterised as ballistic. Studies carried out in the last few years suggest, however, that they may not be.

In recent years cognitive psychologists have shown more interest in the control of action – not in the control of individual muscles, but in how a complex plan of action is represented in the mind and converted into a pattern of muscle movements. Understanding how actions are controlled is complicated by the fact that there are so many ways, at the level of individual muscle movements, of doing the same thing. For example, we are told that we should bend at the knees to pick a heavy object off the floor, not at the waist. So if the plan of action is to pick up a suitcase, there are two main ways of executing that plan – bending primarily at the knees or bending primarily at the waist – and for each of those possibilities there is an endless variety of detailed movements we might make to carry out that plan.

Some ways of picking up a suitcase are more natural than others. Part of the explanation of why they are more natural was suggested by the Russian physiologist N.A. Bernstein. Bernstein suggested that muscles are controlled in groups, and that certain movements are, therefore, difficult to make. For example, it is hard to reach for an object on a table just by bending one's elbow. The natural tendency is for other joints to move in harmony.

Bernstein's idea has been taken up in the West by Michael Turvey and others. Turvey's own account of the control of motor movements is *noncognitive*. His theory is couched in the framework of *ecological psychology*, an approach derived from the work of James J. Gibson. Gibson argued that physical properties of the environment control our behaviour directly without cognitive mediation. One of the most interesting findings that supports such a view of motor control comes from a study by David Lee of how car drivers estimate when and how hard they need to brake. Lee showed that the 'optic flow' in the image of the upcoming road on the retina can be used to control braking without, according to him, any cognitive processes intervening. However, as any driver knows, how hard you need to brake depends on what car you are driving, how heavily loaded it is, and whether its brakes have been adjusted. If knowledge of these factors controls braking – and there is good reason to think that it does – deciding how hard to brake is a cognitive process. Similarly, Lee's analysis ignores the fact that drivers, for example in stock car races, sometimes have goals other than avoiding collisions. So knowledge of the desired outcome also controls motor behaviour, again suggesting a cognitive account.

Gibson's ecological approach is a controversial one, both in motor control and in visual perception, which was Gibson's own primary field of interest. Most psychologists who work on motor control subscribe to a version of a cognitive theory called *schema theory*. Schema theory claims that actions are controlled by rules called schemas, which relate perceptual information and other environmental conditions to desired outcomes. The relevant perceptual information may include, for example, the optic flow parameters that are important in Lee's account of braking. However, in schema theory these parameters are related to other aspects of the environment, such as what type of car one is driving, and desired outcomes via explicit rules.

One focus of psychological research on action has been the nature and acquisition of complex motor skills. Interest in this topic arose in the Second World War, when it became necessary to train soldiers, sailors, and airmen quickly. This early work was atheoretical – the best method of training each skill was selected by trial and error. The results of this research were subsequently useful in ergonomics – the study of how working environments should be designed – but they had little influence in cognitive psychology. Although it did not guide this Second World War work, there was one theory of motor skills available at that time – a behaviourist one. According to the behaviourists a complex motor skill is a sequence of actions linked together as a chain of stimuli and responses. The first action in the chain is triggered by a stimulus that might have both external (environmental) and internal aspects. The outcome of the first action is the stimulus for the second, and so on. However, just as this behaviourist idea of chaining failed as an account of how words are put together to form sentences, it also failed as an account of skilled behaviour.

An example of a complex motor skill that cannot be analysed satisfactorily within the behaviourist framework is playing the piano. Many aspects of skilled piano playing suggest that a cognitive analysis is essential. Most obviously, the performance of a piece of music depends on both perceptual information (looking at the score) and the player's knowledge, for example about who the composer is, what conventions he or she observed in writing scores, and what contemporary conventions there are for playing music by that composer.

More specifically, a piece of music is not a structureless string of notes, and playing it is not a structureless sequence of events (e.g. moving fingers, pressing keys). The structure of the music itself – its division into subjects, phrases, bars and so on – affects the way a piece is performed. Furthermore, the layout of the keyboard means that while the current phrase is being played, the pianist may have to plan a large movement of one or both hands for the next phrase. In short, the performance of a piece of music must reflect its hierarchical structure, and the control of the movements that make up the performance must also reflect that structure.

What do people learn when they acquire motor skills? We talk about *knowing* how to ride a bike, or how to swim, or how to play the piano. But we cannot say what we know when we know these things. Knowing how to ride a bike is not like knowing the names of the rivers that flow into the sea around the coast of England. Psychologists refer to the first kind of knowledge as *procedural knowledge*, and the second as *declarative knowledge*. These two kinds of knowledge are mediated by different brain mechanisms. For example, Clive Waring, the musician who has lost his ability to remember what happened a few minutes ago, can still conduct the choir that he was in charge of before his illness.

Two other puzzling aspects of skill acquisition are its three main phases and the phenomenon of reaching a plateau. In the early stages of learning, one is told explicitly what to do and where one is going wrong. For example, I remember being told how to hold a tennis racquet and how to play forehand and backhand strokes. At first I had to think to myself, 'I want to play a backhand, so I should turn the racquet in my hand'. Later I learned to associate having turned the racquet with playing a (reasonably!) good shot. Finally, though I do not think my tennis ever reached this stage, performance of these low-level skills becomes almost completely automatic. These three stages of skill acquisition have been noted by several authors, though there is little agreement about how they should be explained. Likewise, those frustrating periods when one's performance simply does not improve, no matter how much practice one puts in, remain a mystery.

A final unsolved problem in understanding the acquisition of motor skills is how *knowledge of results* helps to improve performance. The problem is that the knowledge people have is not obviously in a form that can help them perform better. It does not tell them directly what changes to their muscle movements will eliminate the errors they have made. For example, Nigel Harvey studied people learning to sing. Singers produce different notes by various means, including regulating the flow of air from their lungs and altering the shape of their vocal tracts. But they are not conscious of how the air is flowing or of the shape of their vocal tract when they produce a particular note. What they do usually know, either because they themselves can hear or because their singing teachers tell them, is whether the notes sounded right. But how does that information allow them to make the appropriate changes in air flow and vocal tract shape to produce the right note? Harvey argues that knowledge of results in this explicit form is *not* crucial for learning, but that sensory feedback about muscle position is, although people are typically unaware that they are using such feedback. Knowledge of results is useful only when it provides a counterpart to sensory feedback that can be verbalised, and so allows people to talk about their performance. Harvey predicted that singers would continue to improve even when they were not consciously aware of how the notes they produced were different from those intended, and he showed that this prediction was true. This finding reflects the everyday observation that skills are learned primarily by practice, which fine tunes the (largely unconscious) ability to use sensory feedback, and not by explicit verbal instruction.

ROBOT MOTION

Work in artificial intelligence has made a major contribution to our knowledge about movement and action. In particular our understanding of the computations required to find a suitable path around a series of obstacles has benefited greatly from the study of robot motion.

For many people the term robot suggests human- or animal-like creatures, such as R2-D2 and C-3PO in *Star Wars*. However, we also know of industrial robots – advertisers would have us believe that some cars are made by them. An industrial robot is more like a hand and arm than a person. So far two generations of robots have been used in industry. First generation robots can only pick things up and put them down somewhere else. Their movements are controlled by stops. To bring them to a halt you almost literally have to put a spanner in the works. Second generation robots store fixed sequences of actions in memory. These sequences may be learned from a human 'teacher'. For example, robots that spray car bodies can be trained by moving them through the positions they will have to occupy in performing the task. In both types of robot the movements are ballistic.

The long-awaited third generation of intelligent robots will be more versatile. They will know what they are supposed to be doing, and they will monitor their actions *as they perform them* to see if they are getting things right. If they are not, for whatever reason – an unexpected change in their environment, perhaps – they will take steps to correct their errors. Nevertheless, these robots will still not be the metal androids of science fiction. Even to make a 'fixed arm' robot behave intelligently is a difficult task.

If a 'fixed arm' robot is to move intelligently it must work out where it wants its hand to be and how much force it must apply to get it there. The solutions to these problems require results from three branches of mathematics – kinematics, statics, and dynamics – which people are often introduced to at school either in applied mathematics or in physics. Kinematics is about the paths along which things move and how quickly they move along them. There are many ways that a robot can move its hand to a point in its workspace. The problem is to choose a sensible route. This problem is comparatively easy if there is little else in the workspace, but it becomes complicated when there are other objects, particularly if those objects are moving.

A similar problem arises if the robot itself can move, though it is in some ways simpler to solve, since the robot is not attached to anything in the way that a hand is attached to an arm. A free-moving robot needs a certain amount of clearance around each object in its workspace. This idea can be used to work out whether a robot can get through a gap between two objects. However, considerable complications arise if the robot has a complex shape – it may be able to wiggle through a gap that it cannot go directly through.

Statics deals with the forces a robot exerts on its environment, and dynamics with the forces needed to move the robot itself (or the hand of a fixed arm robot). In robot motion the problem to be solved is: given a position, find the forces needed to move the robot to that position.

First and second generation robots have no sense organs, or only rudimentary ones. More intelligent robots might be able to see the world they move about in, and use visual information to guide them through that world, in much the same way that people do. Their mechanical eyes will perform computations similar to those described in chapter 2. However, such robots will have to wait until those computations can be carried out quickly enough to make mechanical eyes viable.

PLANNING ACTIONS

First and second generation robots carry out fixed sequences of actions. More intelligent robots will be able to plan their own actions from a higher-level specification of their tasks. In AI, the creation of a plan is a problem to be solved, and it is usually solved by problem reduction (see chapter 5). The high-level specification of the plan is reduced to a sequence of basic actions that the robot can perform. In the simplest plans, the actions can be carried out in any order. If you want to clean a shelf, it does not matter which things you remove first and which last, provided they are not stacked. Usually, however, it is more efficient to carry out actions in one order rather than another. If you want to make a cup of tea, it is better to put the kettle on first and then find cups and saucers, milk and sugar while it is boiling, rather than finding those things before you put the kettle on. And some actions *must* be carried out before others. You cannot brew tea until you have boiling water, for example.

We plan our everyday actions without difficulty and, unless we become cognitive scientists, we feel no need for an explanation of this ability. However, research in AI has shown that planning, like many of the skills we have looked at in this book, is far from simple.

In chapter 2 we discussed object recognition in the MIT BLOCKSWORLD. Much of the early research on planning looked at the creation of plans in the restricted domain of the BLOCKSWORLD, in the hope that what was learned could be generalised to more interesting cases. BLOCKSWORLD planning programs made plans to stack and restack piles of blocks. To plan a sequence of actions that will stack blocks in a particular way it is necessary to know what the world will be like as each part of the plan is carried out. This obvious fact unexpectedly leads to a difficulty for AI planning systems, the so-called *frame problem*.

In both the BLOCKSWORLD and the real world, actions typically have relatively minor repercussions. Most things stay the same when an action is performed, only a few things change. The repercussions of an action can be compared with the changes from one frame of a cartoon film to the next – almost everything stays the same. Hence, the name 'frame problem'. But what is the problem? The problem is that we need to know what the world is like at each stage in our sequence of actions, but it would be tedious explicitly to redescribe all those aspects of the world that do not change when an action is performed. To be more precise, it would be tedious in the BLOCKSWORLD, but impossible in the real world.

Cordell Green did devise a BLOCKSWORLD planning system in which the frame problem was 'solved' by brute force, but it was very cumbersome. Most subsequent BLOCKSWORLD systems used a technique introduced in a system called STRIPS. What STRIPS does is associate three lists with each basic action: a set of preconditions to be satisfied before the action can be performed, an add list, and a delete list. The add list is a list of statements that become true when the action is performed. The delete list is a list of statements that cease to be true when it is performed. Any aspect of the world not explicitly referred to in the add and delete lists is assumed to be the same in the frame before and the frame after the action is performed.

The fact that actions have preconditions explains why the actions that make up a plan may have to be carried out in a particular order. A modified version of STRIPS, called RSTRIPS, looks ahead to actions still to be performed to make sure that their preconditions can be fulfilled – carrying out one action may irretrievably destroy the preconditions for another. For example, if you are trying to make a meringue and you beat the egg before you separate the yolk from the white, you will have to start again with another egg.

Like STRIPS, RSTRIPS does all its planning at a single level – that of basic actions. In reality, people plan at different levels. Once a problem has been broken up into subproblems, planning can start, even if those subproblems cannot be solved by 'basic actions'. Earl Sacerdoti introduced this idea of hierarchical planning into STRIPS-like systems, and showed that it is more efficient than single-level planning.

One aspect of planning that BLOCKSWORLD systems are effectively able to ignore is resource limitations. For example, if you are making a meringue and you beat the egg white and yolk together, and you haven't got another egg, and it is 8 o'clock on Sunday evening, and you live in a house that stands on its own in the country and your guests are just arriving, you could be in trouble! When making plans, or revising them after a catastrophe, you have to take into account what resources – including sometimes what inner resources – are available to you.

UNDERSTANDING AND EXPLAINING ACTIONS

One of the most difficult problems for cognitive scientists is to explain how people explain their own and other people's actions. It is a problem that has exercised philosophers for centuries, but cognitive science has already made some distinctive contributions to solving it.

In explaining actions, a distinction must be made between reasons for actions and causes of them. The distinction is a problematic one. Indeed, many philosophers have denied it exists – they have claimed that all reasons for action are also causes of action (though not the converse). In paradigmatic cases the identification of reason and cause is a reasonable one. If I have run out of bread, I have a reason for going to the baker's or to the supermarket. My thinking that I am out of bread, together with my background knowledge about where bread is sold, is one of the factors that produces the motion of my body in the direction of the supermarket – it is one of the causes of my going there.

However, despite the fact that my reason for performing an action is often causally effective in my carrying it out, there is a conceptual distinction between reasons and causes. What causes an action must be determined objectively, but if you want to know the reason why someone did something, you have to ask them. In this sense, a person is the final authority on the reasons for their actions – if they say they did something for a particular reason, that's why they did it. Of course, people sometimes lie – they may want to hide their real reasons for acting. But lying is not restricted to lying about reasons for action and there are ways of telling when someone is lying, even if they are not foolproof.

In our post-Freudian world, it is commonly claimed that people often hide the real reasons for their actions from themselves. In my view, this idea is misleading. In some cases, such as obsessive hand-washing, there is no good reason for what a person does, though there might be understandable causes. The reason the person gives seems valid to them – they have touched something dirty, for example – but objectively it is not. Obsessive hand-washers also, typically, fail to understand why their obsession developed – they do not know what caused their condition. Other cases, for example when someone denies that their obsequious behaviour is aimed at securing a promotion, are harder to assess, though denying the true reason for an action can often be explained by the fact that that reason is socially unacceptable.

There is a further complication in assessing reasons for action. The reason for carrying out a purposeful action may not be explicitly before the mind of the person doing it. For example, if you are driving along a suburban street chatting to a passenger and a child runs out in front of the car, you very quickly move your foot from the accelerator to the brake and, you hope, avert an accident. Why did you stamp on the brake? To stop the car, of course. Did that reason flash through your mind as the child ran out? Very probably not. You acted automatically. Philosophers have used the term *intention in action* to describe this phenomenon. Your act was not unintentional – you meant to stop. But your intention to stop (or equivalently for present purposes your reason for stopping) was not 'in your mind' as you carried out the action. It was expressed, in the first instance, in the action itself. A consequence of the phenomenon of intention in action is that when people give reasons for their actions, they often have to 'reconstruct' them after the event. Such reconstructed reasons are not causes of actions in the same way that my thinking to myself 'I'm out of bread' is a cause of my going to the supermarket.

In the simple case of trying to stop the car there is little doubt that the reconstructed reason is correct, but matters are not always so straightforward. People do not like to think that they have acted irrationally (i.e. without good reason). So if they are asked to give a reason for something they have done, they would rather say something plausible than admit that they do not know why they did what they did. Since reasons often have to be reconstructed, and since folk psychology can be used in this process of reconstruction, it is not surprising that people can give reasons for their actions that bear little relation to why they did what they did.

We all know that people rationalise. They construct, after the event, an explanation of what they have done that makes it look sensible and motivated. Rationalisation is more common than we usually take it to be. The cases that come to our attention usually have some insidious feature, so to say that someone has rationalised is often to make a critical comment. The other, unnoticed, cases are mainly harmless. However, people like to think, and they like others to think, that they have good reasons for behaving the way they do. Nevertheless, the reasons they give have not always guided their actions in the way they would like to believe.

Since an intention to act is often an intention in action, and the corresponding reason a reason in action, how can we substantiate the claim that someone has not given a genuine reason for their actions? Sometimes the fact that they are rationalising is obvious. However, there are experimental methods that can uncover rationalisations where they might not be suspected. For example, in chapter 5 we introduced Peter Wason's selection task and said that one account of why people fail to solve this problem is that they simply pick cards mentioned in the rule. However, if people are asked why they picked a card, they almost never say because it was explicitly mentioned. They rationalise their choices. That their explanations are rationalisations is shown by the facts that they are equally confident in explaining correct and incorrect choices, and that the methods of choosing cards that they report for these two cases are based on incompatible criteria. Jonathan Evans made a strong case that these explanations *do not reflect the reasons for people's choices*. He showed that the pattern of choices for people who could not solve the selection task could be explained, as we have already mentioned, on the assumption that they pick cards that are mentioned directly in the rule.

Some writers, in particular Richard Nisbett and Timothy Wilson, have concluded that people have no (or almost no) introspective access to the cognitive processes that underlie their actions. According to Nisbett and Wilson, even when people are right about the reasons for their actions, it is not because they can look into their minds and see how they decided what to do. If Nisbett and Wilson are right, how do people give reasons for their actions, and why are those reasons often correct? According to Nisbett and Wilson, all reason-giving is rational reconstruction. However, since much of the folk psychology on which this reconstruction is based is correct, our reasons are often right too, particularly when the influences on our behaviour are salient and come readily to mind as possible causes of our behaviour.

Nisbett and Wilson's account of simple cases, such as buying bread, seems unnecessarily complex. When I explain why I went to the supermarket, do I really base my reasoning on folk psychological knowledge about when people go shopping rather than on knowledge of how I decided to make that particular shopping trip? Nevertheless, Nisbett and Wilson review a large number of empirical findings that suggest there are many cases in which people have very poor insight into the factors that influence their behaviour.

For example, if insomniacs are given a pill that they are told either produces or reduces symptoms that are typical of insomnia, such as rapid heart rate and alertness, they take, respectively, a shorter and a longer time to fall asleep. The obvious explanation is that subjects who are told that the pill produces the symptoms attribute the symptoms to the pill rather than to their worries, whereas the subjects who are told that the pill reduces the symptoms feel that their worries are particularly acute, since they suffer the symptoms even after taking the pill. In fact, the pills were always inert placebos. In a subsequent interview almost no one attributed their ease or difficulty in falling asleep to the pill. Rather, they talked about the acuteness or otherwise of their worries. Indeed, when presented with the 'obvious' explanation most subjects rejected it.

This example also supports Nisbett and Wilson's claim that when trying to explain our own or other people's behaviour we give too much weight to things that come readily to mind (e.g. what we were worrying about) and too little to less obvious influences (e.g. the fact that we have taken a pill). A further example, from everyday life, is the depression that is often associated with premenstrual tension. Some women, who are perfectly well aware of the connection between this depression and their monthly cycle, nevertheless find it difficult to accept that it is not caused by bad things that have been happening to them.

In another study Nisbett and Wilson asked people in a shop which of four (identical) pairs of stockings they thought was best. The pair on the far right was chosen much more frequently than the pair on the far left even though, when they were asked to explain their choices, no one mentioned position, which, indeed, ought to have been irrelevant. When asked if position had affected their choice, people 'denied it, usually with a worried glance at the interviewer suggesting that they felt either that they had misunderstood the question or were dealing with a madman'.

I will mention just one more study discussed by Nisbett and Wilson. In a classic experiment on problem solving, N. Maier asked people to tie together the ends of two strings hanging from the ceiling too far apart for both to be reached at the same time. Maier was interested in the solution in which a handy object is tied onto one string, which is then set swinging like a pendulum while the other is pulled towards it. Maier's solution was a difficult one, which most people failed to see until he 'accidentally' brushed against one string and set it swinging. For Nisbett and Wilson the most interesting aspect of Maier's findings was that hardly anyone mentioned his brushing against the string when asked how they had come to think of the solution. Even under more intense questioning, only about one third of them mentioned it. Furthermore, if Maier had twirled an object around as well as brushing the string, they said that the twirling had suggested the solution. But people who had only seen a weight being twirled almost never solved the problem.

Despite the fact that Nisbett and Wilson's claims are too strong, the findings they discuss show that people's explanations of their own behaviour – the reasons they give for doing things – are often inaccurate. Reasons are not always causes. They are often rationalisations that play no role in producing the behaviour that they putatively explain.

Another important observation, related to Nisbett and Wilson's claims, is that when giving explanations of our own behaviour we tend to focus on aspects of the situation we are in, but when giving explanations of other people's behaviour we tend to stress character traits. So I might say that I failed to give a tip in a restaurant because the service was poor or because I didn't have any change, but I might say that you didn't because you are mean. Although both internal (character traits) and external factors are important influences on behaviour, we cannot be right about both ourselves and others if we stress situational factors as producing our own behaviour and character traits as producing other people's. Social psychologists argue that the primary reason for this *actor–observer difference* is that other people's dispositions are overemphasised in our explanations of their behaviour. They call this mistake the *fundamental attribution error*. This error provides yet another reason for regarding the relation between explanations and causes of behaviour as an indirect one.

FURTHER READING

There is no obvious introductory reference on the cognitive science of action. The way we explain our own and other people's behaviour is discussed in detail by Richard Nisbett and Lee Ross in *Human Inference: Strategies and Shortcomings of Social Judgement* (Prentice-Hall, 1980).

8　Understanding ourselves

We all feel a need to understand the world we live in, and there are many ways we can try to understand it. Science provides a special kind of understanding, as evidenced by the changes in our environment it makes possible. It is not the only way of understanding the world, and it does not explain everything. Nor is scientific knowledge an unalloyed good. However, for good or bad, science makes a radical difference to our world view and to our lives.

Just as we take our mental apparatus for granted, and fail to see the need for a cognitive science, we take for granted those aspects of our environment that are made possible by scientific understanding, and forget what we owe to them. At the most basic level, many of us would not be here without the medical treatment that science and technology have made possible. A high proportion of children used to die during childbirth, and an alarming number of mothers, too. And even those children who survived their first year had a high chance of dying in later childhood. In my own case, if I had survived childhood, and avoided such diseases of early adulthood as tuberculosis, I would almost certainly have been claimed by appendicitis, complicated by severe peritonitis, a few years ago. There may be aspects of modern medicine that we do not like, and that deserve criticism, but we should never forget what we owe it.

To take another example, most readers of this book will find it hard to conceive of life without mains electricity, and the electrical appliances that are now so readily available. Yet the electric motor has only been with us for about 150 years, washing machines, vacuum cleaners and the rest for less. All these products are a result, if often only an indirect one, of a scientific approach to natural phenomena. Although it would be absurd to suggest that we fully understand the physical world, the physical sciences are well developed. They allow a detailed explanation of phenomena in our immediate environment and, in many cases, well beyond it. No one who gives any thought to the matter can doubt that these sciences provide profound insights into the nature and workings of the physical world.

But what about the animal world and, more specifically, the human world? Many people have doubts about the ability of science to explain some facts about human life. Many applications of science to biological phenomena are, of course, non-controversial – the biological sciences are well established and have produced important ideas and applications. The discovery of the microbial causes of infection and of vaccines for smallpox and other infectious diseases are examples. However, two aspects of human life have always seemed difficult to explain scientifically. The first is its origin. The second is that people have minds.

Until the nineteenth century people were sceptical about a scientific account of the origins of life because they could not imagine what form it might take. Darwin and Wallace's theory of evolution changed that. If, within a population, organisms have varying characteristics, if those characteristics are (at least partially) inherited, if certain characteristics make some organisms better suited for survival (and reproduction) than others, and if there are not enough resources for all the organisms to survive, the characteristics of the population can change over time. That is the essence of the theory of evolution. It provides the framework for a detailed account of how living organisms arose and evolved. For example, the *mechanism* of inheritance was first described by Mendel in his theory of (what were later called) genes, and its detailed biochemistry has been uncovered by twentieth-century molecular biologists. Whether creationists like it or not, the theory of evolution shows that a scientific account of the origin of life is possible, though it has nothing to say about the origin of the inorganic matter from which life arose.

Cognitive science addresses itself to the major outstanding problem for the scientific understanding of living organisms: how can mental phenomena be explained? Historically, this understanding has been hampered by dualism, an important strand of Western thinking about the mind, which originated in its modern form with the French philosopher, René Descartes. Dualists hold that mind and matter are distinct. They, therefore, have to explain how events in the mental and material worlds are related – a problem that they have never convincingly solved. Dualism is not incompatible with a science of cognition – that science could be completely separate from the physical sciences. However, with its discoveries about the relation between mental events and the nervous system, cognitive science makes implausible the idea that mental and material phenomena require different kinds of explanation. Cognitive scientists believe that to say a person, an animal, or perhaps even a machine, has a mind is not to say that it has some non-material part, but to say that it is capable of behaving in certain ways: of perceiving, remembering, using language, thinking, learning, and acting. Furthermore, the theory of evolution suggests that animals have evolved from inorganic (and, hence, material) origins. It would go against the spirit of that theory to suggest that at some point in the course of evolution a non-material mind miraculously appeared.

It is one thing to say that the mind can be explained in material terms, but quite another to develop a detailed explanation of it. The theory of evolution solved the problem of explaining the material origins of life. Is there a similarly fundamental idea in cognitive science that forms the basis of a material explanation of the mind? The best candidate is the thesis suggested by the mathematician Alan Turing: *every effective procedure can be described in computational terms.* We mentioned in chapter 1 that Turing and other mathematicians had shown that any mathematically interesting computation, in the very broad sense of that term, can be analysed into basic building blocks and carried out automatically by a machine. If anything a 'biological machine' can do can be characterised as a computation (Turing's thesis), any cognitive process is a process that could be carried out by a machine. On this view, the cognitive processes of man and other animals are compatible with a unified scientific approach to the natural world.

The discussion so far has been abstract. What are its implications for the way we understand ourselves? It is a commonplace to say that science has undermined our idea of human beings as the centre of the universe. The physical sciences show we are not at the physical centre of the universe. Indeed, the idea of a physical centre is no longer as clear as it once seemed to be. What is clear, however, is that the Earth has no special position in the universe. In biology, the theory of evolution shows that we are not the ultimate form of life or the end product of a process of development that is now complete. Evolution is not a purposeful process and it has no goal. The idea that life can evolve from material origins dethrones us in another way. It suggests that there could be life elsewhere in the universe, a topic about which there has been much speculation, though there is no satisfactory way of estimating the relevant probabilities.

Cognitive science helps us to understand ourselves as part of the general order of things. Just as the theory of evolution shows how things as complicated as people could arise by purely natural processes from inorganic matter, admittedly over a very long time, cognitive science shows us how perception, memory, the use of language, thinking, learning, and acting can be understood in purely mechanical terms. In this sense, cognitive science shows that, at least for the cognitive aspects of our mental life, we do not need a dualist account. The mental can be explained in material terms.

In a sense this idea is a reductionist one – seeing, remembering, thinking, learning, and acting are physical events. However, this reductionism amounts only to the claim that mental processes are *ultimately* mediated in a way that can be understood in physical terms. It does not imply that mental events ought to be explained using only the vocabulary of physics. We need a mental vocabulary not only for everyday explanations of behaviour but also for scientific ones. Just as evolutionary theorists retain their specialised concepts, though they believe that evolution is a physical process, so cognitive scientists will need to retain psychological concepts *as an essential part of their theoretical apparatus.* Even within the physical sciences, chemists, for example, or astronomers have their own specialised concepts, though they know that the phenomena they study are physical in nature and, hence, can be *reduced* to basic physics. Rejecting dualism does *not* mean that cognitive science should, or even can, be replaced by physics.

Darwin and Wallace's account of the basic mechanism of evolution was the most important advance toward a theory of the origins of life. However, detailed explanations of particular facts are important both in lending the theory credence and in giving it a particular form. Darwin himself was led to the theory by his observations of speciation, particularly in the Galapagos Islands. This work included detailed case studies of the adaptation of the Galapagos finches to the environments on the different islands, for example. Similarly, the work in molecular genetics that uncovered the detailed mechanism of genetic inheritance has fleshed out the theory, and given it greater plausibility.

Cognitive science also needs both a general framework for producing explanations of our cognitive abilities – the computational framework provided by Turing's thesis – and in-depth analyses of those abilities – analyses of the kind we have outlined in chapters 2 to 7. These detailed analyses suggest, in a more direct way than the general framework, the sense in which cognitive science helps us to understand ourselves.

Looking back over these chapters, it transpires that the ways these analyses help us to understand ourselves range from the straightforward to the problematic. The case of the senses, for example, is a straightforward one. Normally people do not worry about how they see or hear things. But with a bit of persuasion most people, particularly if they know something of the elementary physics of light and sound, realise that there is much to be explained about sight and hearing. Within cognitive science there are highly technical accounts of how we see and hear, and much controversy about which account is correct. However, in vision in particular, thanks in large part to the work of Marr, there is reasonable agreement about the kinds of computations that turn patterns of light and dark (Marr's grey-level descriptions) into representations of the people and objects in the world around us.

Understanding the way we see is rather like understanding the way we digest food – it is unlikely to have any great effect on the way we conduct our lives. However, the same cannot be said for other cognitive functions. Here our folk psychological understanding of ourselves is more likely to be upset. Take memory, for example. Cognitive science shows that our memories can be unreliable in unexpected ways, and when we least expect them to be. For example, they can be inaccurate even when they seem particularly vivid, as studies of 'flashbulb' memories have shown. And the unreliability, often systematic, of eyewitness testimony has important implications for the way we should interpret courtroom testimony, at least if we want to find out the truth.

From the point of view of understanding ourselves, the impact of the cognitive science of adult language use has been more like that of the study of perception than the study of memory, though the study of language acquisition has produced some surprises. Understanding the mechanics of word recognition or the way that the literal meaning of a sentence is put together from the meanings of its parts might help us to build machines that understand language. It might, eventually, help us to help people who have problems with language. But it will not make us reassess the folk psychology of language, because there is no folk psychology of those aspects of language use. However, future developments are likely to challenge some of our preconceptions, for example about how accurately we typically understand what is said to us. And the controversy that has surrounded attempts to teach language to apes indicates the importance of that research for the way we think about ourselves.

We do not need cognitive science to tell us that human reasoning is fallible. What it can give us is a more accurate account of the circumstances under which people reason badly. Here it may produce surprises, as well as pointers to the way we should think about ourselves. If we understood better when and why people reasoned badly, we would be alerted to circumstances in which they might have made crucial errors. If we knew when we ourselves were likely to make mistakes, we might be more modest in some of our claims. And we might be more aware of when other people are trying to make us draw the wrong conclusion by, for example, using persuasive rather than valid arguments, or getting us to accept their view of the facts by a seemingly authoritative statement of those facts. A proper understanding of how people think could have important consequences for, for example, resisting propaganda.

There are many other cases in which it is important to anticipate human error. I will mention just one example. The idea of a universal computing machine was conceived in the last century by Charles Babbage, who was thwarted in his ambitions of building it by the cumbersome nature of the mechanical components he was forced to use. His idea arose out of an earlier project in which he had designed a machine for computing tables of logarithms. Nowadays we take tables of logarithms and scientific calculators with log functions for granted. In the early nineteenth century log tables were produced by teams of error-prone human 'computers'. Errors in these tables were serious, because log tables were used for navigation and an error in the tables could lead to an error in setting a course, sometimes with fatal consequences. A better understanding of when human computers were likely to make errors would have made it possible to produce more accurate log tables.

It hardly needs saying that a better understanding of how people learn has, at least potentially, important consequences for education and study at all levels. Unfortunately, as we saw in chapter 6, the cognitive science of learning is not as well developed as some other branches of the discipline. However, it seems certain, given the problems people have in devising successful education systems, that a well-developed cognitive science of learning will upset many of our folk psychological assumptions. Furthermore, having a folk theory can make learning more difficult. Incorrect naive theories about electricity, for example, often underlie errors make by physics students when they are solving problems. Educators not only have to teach students new material, they also have to know how and why students' appreciation of new ideas will be affected by what they already know or think they know.

In its attempts to explain behaviour, cognitive science focuses on what happens in individual minds. It is best suited to explaining behaviour that depends on the individual and on those aspects of the world that can readily be internalised and mentally represented. But which are these aspects of behaviour? The topics in this book give an implicit, if partial, answer to this question. Seeing the world, identifying words, solving puzzles, and playing board games are clear cases. However, one question that some readers may have asked themselves is: what about social behaviour? What has cognitive science to say about that?

Traditionally, social psychology has been separate from cognitive (or, historically, human experimental) psychology, though a recent approach within social psychology is referred to as 'cognitive'. And AI has had little, if anything, to say about social behaviour. In fact, some critics have suggested that AI can never explain intelligent behaviour, because all such behaviour has a social component, and because computers have no social life. This criticism has little force against, say, computer models of early visual processing, which has no social aspect, but it does raise questions about, for example, whether computers can ever be said to understand language, no matter how complex the manipulations of linguistic symbols that they perform.

Within psychology there are long-standing debates about both the correct method of studying social behaviour and the types of explanation appropriate to it. One view is that social behaviour should be studied experimentally, like any other behaviour. There are two objections to this idea. The first is contentious and states that the experimental approach has not produced theoretically important insights into social behaviour. The second holds that experimenting on social behaviour affects it in such complex ways that it is impossible to conclude anything from social psychological experiments. Alternatives to the experimental approach include observing, or otherwise collecting data on, social behaviour in its natural setting, asking participants in social interactions to give accounts of them 'after the event', and detailed study of the vocabulary used to describe social behaviour.

However one studies social behaviour, the question remains of how it should be explained. Cognitive science suggests that, insofar as social behaviour is governed by social conventions, rules and norms, those norms will be represented in the minds of the individual members of society. These representations not only play a causal role in our own social behaviour, they also affect the way we understand other people's social behaviour. From this perspective the explanation of social behaviour should be another aspect of cognitive science. Yet as the contents of this book show, it is not in practice. Why not?

There is no simple answer to this question, but the following three points are relevant. First, societies, and the conventions by which they conduct their affairs, have complexities that we find difficult to discern and to describe. Because these conventions are not readily apparent, it is difficult to formulate a theory, cognitive or otherwise, about social behaviour. Even if a cognitive science of that behaviour is possible, it will be a hard task constructing it.

Second, the relation between social conventions and what is in people's minds is not so straightforward as the corresponding relation for other aspects of behaviour. For example, everyone's visual system must embody the generalisations that Marr identified as crucial in visual processing – the assumption, for example, that surfaces in the world tend to be continuous (see p. 28). Or again, all literate speakers of English have in their minds information about what common English words look like in print. For complex social conventions the same argument cannot be made, particularly when those conventions are not, and may never be, explicitly formulated. People often have only a partial, or even an incorrect, understanding of social conventions. This observation does not rule out a cognitive science of social behaviour, but it does indicate that it must be more complex than, for example, the cognitive science of seeing.

Third, for many aspects of social behaviour people do not internalise, in any straightforward sense, the factors that influence them. This observation applies in particular to those parts of social psychology that are more akin to sociology than cognitive science. For example, having an alcoholic parent may have serious and, to some extent, predictable effects on a child's development, yet the child may have no concept of alcoholism, let alone have internalised the fact that its parent is alcoholic.

CONSCIOUSNESS

One of the most striking aspects of our mental life is that we are conscious of the things we see or hear or think about. We can even be conscious of (some of) our mental processes and of ourselves. Indeed, without consciousness there is no mental *life*, only mental processing. What does cognitive science have to say about consciousness? In my own view, very little, though some cognitive scientists have said a lot about it. It is hard to know what questions cognitive science might ask about consciousness. Indeed, in their search for questions about consciousness, cognitive scientists sometimes confuse it with related notions such as awareness, which is a more general concept, or self-consciousness, which is a more specific one.

One popular idea is that cognitive science might consider the evolutionary question, why should animals that are conscious be favoured over those that are not by natural selection? This question is impossible to answer, for the following reason. Consider a putative answer: for example, consciousness allows an animal to experience pain and, hence, to take appropriate action when it is injured. Now ask the further question, why could not an animal without consciousness possess the same advantage? If it behaved in exactly the same way – if it reacted appropriately when injured – what extra benefit could the experience of pain confer? There is no obvious answer – indeed, from this point of view, pain seems to have negative value. So consciousness remains a mystery.

9   Final word

Cognitive science is the scientific study of cognition. Its aim is to explain our cognitive abilities, and not primarily to document 'interesting facts' about cognition. Cognitive scientists study perceiving and knowing, and ancillary activities such as remembering, paying attention, manipulating the environment, and language use. However, my goal has not been to list the topics that cognitive scientists study, but to give a feel for the scientific approach to cognition. To understand cognitive science is to understand what sorts of questions cognitive scientists ask about perceiving and knowing, and what kinds of answer they expect to find. In this last chapter, I return to three general themes that have recurred throughout the book.

The first is that the explanations of cognitive science are different from everyday explanations of the same phenomena. The reasons for this difference lie in the different purposes of everyday and scientific explanations, and the different background assumptions against which they operate. In our ordinary lives we assume, for example, that people can reach out and pick up small objects close to them. Only deviations from this norm need to be explained: the object is unexpectedly heavy, or it is stuck down, or the person is paralysed. The first step toward cognitive science is to realise that even straightforward cases of reaching out and picking up an object – ones that ordinarily need no explanation – depend on the analysis of complex visual information entering the eyes and on finely controlled and coordinated motor movements. Science attempts to explain natural phenomena, including those that need no everyday explanation, using general principles that are empirically testable, and cognitive science is no exception. It attempts, in this case, to provide an account of the *mechanisms*, in the most general sense of that term, that underlie our ability to guide our hands towards objects, to grasp them, and to pick them up. Cognitive science has to cash mechanistic metaphors for the mind, and to show that they need not be degrading or undermine human values. It has to cash them because, if our current ideas are correct, we will not be able to explain mental phenomena at all if we cannot explain them using the general (Turing machine) concept of mechanism.

All explanations come to an end: everyday explanations with everyday facts we can take for granted; scientific explanations with general principles we cannot yet explain further. In either case, the actual point at which an explanation comes to an end can change. In everyday life, new norms are established – almost everyone in the Western world now has a television. In science two things happen. First, we replace less general principles by more general ones. Second, we try to show how, in principle, explanations in a less basic science fit with those in a more basic one. The chemical properties of atoms and molecules are explained by their physical properties, biological phenomena are explained biochemically, and so on. Because the fit is only an 'in principle' one – biological explanations, for example, are not reduced in any practical sense to biochemical ones – we do not do away with biology. Similarly, cognitive scientists hope to see how, in principle, cognitive mechanisms are compatible with a neurophysiological description of the brain. Not that they will ever want to, or be able to, dispense with a psychological level of explanation, but they can be more confident that the explanations of cognitive science are mechanistic if they can see how the mind might be embodied in the brain.

The second point I want to return to is how a scientific account of cognition should be evaluated. Many everyday explanations can be evaluated 'on the spot'. We can often decide, for example, whether a person is blind. If they are, we can explain why they cannot see things we would otherwise expect them to see. The generalisations that underlie everyday explanations, for example that blind people cannot see, have 'stood the test of time' and are rarely questioned. That is part of what is meant by saying that they belong to folk theory, though, as we have seen several times, folk theory is not always correct. More generally, and sometimes fortunately for our survival, everyday methods for deciding whether something is true typically produce immediate answers (Do I like these curtains? Is the weather too bad for a picnic? Will this sabre-toothed tiger eat me if I don't run away?). Even when we cannot make an immediate judgement for ourselves, we assume that an expert would be able to make such a judgement. However, immediate judgements typically provide no information about the mechanisms that produce them.

In cognitive science, on the other hand, as in any other science, explanations are couched in terms of mechanisms underlying, for example, our ability to use language, and ideas about those mechanisms cannot be evaluated by whether they seem right or sound plausible. In particular the generalisations of a science – its hypotheses, laws and theories – cannot be taken for granted in the way that folk psychology can be. Their consequences have to be worked out, in the form of predictions about specific facts that should be true if the generalisations are. Those predictions then have to be tested empirically. If the predictions are true the theory might be true, if they are false the theory is definitely wrong. Furthermore, generalisations should be formulated precisely, so that anyone, not just the person who had the ideas, can work out what their consequences are.

Science has adopted, and built on, a way of thinking that we use all the time: when we make a factual claim it ought to be checked against empirical evidence. If the claim is a general one, this checking process is difficult, because many different bits of evidence may be relevant. However, people are not very good at checking their general claims – we all have our prejudices and we do not always follow Oliver Cromwell's dictum: think it possible you may be mistaken.

The foregoing is not to say that there is *a* scientific method. If there were a formula telling us how to do cognitive science, it would be easier, but less interesting. However, to be scientific is to commit oneself to formulating explanations that can, and should, be evaluated objectively. Of course, scientists do not put forward ideas and straightaway try to show they are wrong. Usually, it is other scientists who try to disprove our ideas. However, part of being scientific is to formulate one's ideas so that there are clear criteria for deciding whether they are right or wrong.

In our everyday lives we are rarely called upon to be as objective as scientists. And it can be particularly difficult to see the need for an objective analysis of, say, decision making. We are directly aware of what is running through our minds when we make decisions, so how can someone tell us we are wrong? In one sense they cannot, because we have privileged access to our thoughts. But a scientific analysis of how people make decisions shows that this privileged access is not the same as having special knowledge about the factors that influence our behaviour. Cognitive scientists are likely to tell us two things about decision making. First, the thoughts running through our minds are often less directly related to our decisions than we think they are. Second, things that are not running through our minds – that we are not aware of – influence our decisions. When choosing groceries, for example, we may know what we have run out of, and need to replace. However, we may be partly or completely unaware of the way that packaging influences our choice of what we buy.

Scientific conclusions are provisional and assailable. People feel uneasy with them. They prefer certainty. Indeed, in those areas of everyday life where objective evaluations are called for, we are often unhappy with such evaluations, especially if they are inconclusive. When we know we cannot expect to know something ourselves, we refer to experts, who should know. Our lack of empathy with the scientific approach explains, in part, our ambivalent feelings toward doctors and other professionals. On the one hand we expect them to have answers to our questions. On the other hand we are irritated by their fallibility, because we do not always understand why they make mistakes. A better understanding of scientific objectivity would allow us to formulate better (everyday) explanations of why they are fallible. It would also give us (and, with luck, them, too!) insight into how they could do better.

A third theme in this book has been that the intellectual content of cognitive science lies primarily in its theories, not in the facts it has discovered about cognition. As in any other science, empirical investigations in cognitive science reveal new facts that subsequent theories have to explain. Although science starts by trying to explain everyday facts in a new way, it soon finds other facts to explain. However, cognitive scientists should not allow themselves to be distracted by 'interesting' facts. If necessary, they have to investigate what are in themselves quite boring matters, if they have important theoretical consequences. To take an example from another science, the precise amount by which light from distant stars is deflected from its course as it passes by the sun is of little significance in itself (and, as it happens, it is minute). However, the measurement of this deflection provided a crucial test of Einstein's general theory of relativity. What could have been a very boring fact gained importance because of its relation to the predictions of a far reaching and revolutionary physical theory.

The theories of cognitive science are important for two main reasons. First, they satisfy the intellectual challenge of providing a general explanation of our cognitive abilities – they show how the last major obstacle to a scientific understanding of the world can be removed. They help us to understand our own nature – our place in the universe, to be more grandiose. Second, unlike other complex explanatory systems developed by mankind over the ages, science allows us to control our environment in a way that has led to the technological developments we take for granted in Western society. If we knew how the mind works, we would be in a better position to help people with cognitive deficits. And if individuals knew how their minds worked, they could avoid the mental manipulation to which they are often subjected.

Index

rationalism 87–9
reasons and causes 106
receptor cells 10, 23–5,
reconstructive memory 51–2
reductionism 19, 113–14
representativeness 82–3
robot motion 103–4
RSTRIPS 105–6
Rubik's cube 70
Rumelhart, David 66, 93

Sacerdoti, Earl 106
Samuel, Arthur 90
schema theory (of action) 101
scientific explanations 1–2, 4, 6–21,
    119–20
scripts 42
segmentation problem 34–6
sensory memory 44–5
serial position effect 43
Shallice, Tim 44
shape from shading 29–31
short-term store (STS) 42–5
SHRDLU 16
sidedness reasoning 35
Skinner, B.F. 19, 87, 88, 89, 95
smell 39
social psychology 116–18
speech errors 62–3
Sperling, George 44–5
state-action method 70–2, 74–5
stereopsis 26–8
STRIPS 105–6
structure from motion 28–9
supervised learning 92, 93–5
Sussman, Gerald 94

syllogisms 77–8

taste 38–9
thinking 68–85, 115
THOG problem 80–1
3-D model description (Marr) 31
Tinbergen, Niko 88
touch 39
Tower of Hanoi 72–3
Turing, Alan 20, 113
Turing machines 20–1, 120
Turing's thesis 113–14
Turvey, Michael 100
Tversky, Amos 82–3
2½D sketch (Marr) 26–31
2–4–6 sketch (Marr) 26–31

Ullman, Shimon 29

Vicki (chimp) 65
vision 6, 8–9, 10–11, 22–36, 52, 114

Wallace, A.R. 112, 114
Waltz, David 35
Waring, Clive 5, 41, 43–4
Warrington, Elizabeth 44
Washoe (chimp) 65
Wason, Peter 78–82
Wason selection task 78–80
Watson, J.B. 19, 87
Wilson, Timothy 108–10
Winograd, Terry 15
Winston, Patrick 93–4
working memory 45

XCON 83